NOMFICTION
a nonfiction anthology about food

NOMFICTION

a nonfiction anthology about food

LITTLE BIG
FICTION TRUTHS

2015 • littlefiction.com

Published by Inkshares Inc., San Francisco, California, as part of the
Little Fiction | Big Truths Collection
www.inkshares.com

Edited by Amanda Leduc and Troy Palmer.
Editorial assistance provided by Vanessa Christensen

Cover design by Troy Palmer.
Images from The Noun Project (thenounproject.com)

ISBN: 9781941758953
e-ISBN: 9781941758960
Library of Congress Control Number: 2016930478

First edition

Printed in the United States of America

NOMFICTION

2015 LITTLE FICTION | BIG TRUTHS

Edited by Amanda Leduc and Troy Palmer. Editorial assistance provided by Vanessa Christensen. Cover design by Troy Palmer. Images from The Noun Project (thenounproject.com)

Publication Credits:

Jessica Kluthe's "Recipe for a Vegetarian" originally appeared in the anthology *EAT IT: Sex, Food & Women's Writing* (2013, Feathertale Press).

A slightly different version of Angela Palm's "The Devolution of Cake" appears online at Little Fiction | Big Truths and was originally published there in 2013.

littlefiction.com

inkshares.com

THE MENU

APÉRITIFS

"Introduction"
served by Amanda Leduc | 9

MAIN COURSES

INTRODUCTION

by Amanda Leduc

THE idea for a food anthology started simply enough: with a typo. While going through submissions to Big Truth's regular stream, I kept mistyping my title as *Nomfiction Editor*. (Thankfully—or not?—I managed to catch the typos before hitting "send".)

Nomfiction, I'd think. *That sounds delicious*. And then I'd go eat pizza, or—more often than not—scrounge around in my fridge for whatever was available. When I went back to my computer, the typo kept on coming. Eventually, a nonfiction anthology about food just seemed like the right thing to do.

But an anthology about food, as it turns out, is anything but simple. We wanted stories about the stuff that goes into our bellies, and we got them. We also got stories about racial tensions, mother-daughter relationships, five-fingered utensils, family recipes, death, the ex-pat existence, and the moldy consequences of ditching school lunches, among others. In short—stories about all the stuff that goes into our hearts, too.

There are sixteen delicious pieces in this collection, and we here at Little Fiction | Big Truths are thrilled and so proud to showcase them all. Like food itself, these essays are comforting and challenging. They are also, by turns, scrumptious and gruesome and sad and queasy-making, and everything else in between. They show us the many different things that sustain us in addition to food— love and hope and joy and anger and sometimes even grief. Each essay, in its way, is a reminder of what it means to be alive.

Dig in. We're sure you'll find them all delicious.

Amanda Leduc

Non-Fiction Editor, Little Fiction | Big Truths

ARANCINI

by Deb Fleischman

IN Italy, *La Madonna* is everywhere—rendered in frescos, enshrined in basilicas, honored in local festivals, invoked in the prayers of old widows and the curses of old men. Even so, a traveler, taken in by the cobblestone piazzas, the art, the hillsides teeming with olive orchards and vineyards, the lyrical language, local wines and regional dishes, might find it easy to forget that this country is Catholic.

It is Christmastime when you and your future husband, Nick, take an overnight train from Umbria in central Italy to Sicily to visit his eighty-two-year-old great-uncle Jo. Jo greets you at the train with a bag of *arancini*, a Sicilian specialty—deep fried, conical rice croquettes stuffed with ground meat, tomato sauce, peas, and mozzarella. They are strange looking but delicious temptations you come to love.

You spend two weeks calling Jo *Zio*, because he is everyone's uncle, the oldest living member of his family on both sides. Three times a day Jo brews shots of espresso, which you sip from tiny porcelain cups in his cramped kitchen, the only room he feels comfortable in. The *cucina* is spare save for an old army cot where he sleeps and the two iconic features of the twenty-first century Italian kitchen—a painting of *La Madonna*, and a TV blaring game shows with half naked go-go dancers. They keep Jo company in his old age, but now he has visitors to entertain.

"Sit down," he gestures, setting out warm homemade ricotta for breakfast—from his friend who makes it fresh, he tells you, "from the cow." Then he lights his pipe and fills the room with Baralo-scented *Forte* tobacco and stories of his youth—the time the whole town came out to corral Glauco's escaped pigs, which were running wild through the *Centro*; his high school field trip up Mt. Etna on Christmas day where he ventured onto steaming pebbles of cooling lava and burned a hole in the sole of his only pair of shoes; Sundays, after church, when he and his pals paraded down Piazza del Duomo, dressed in their finest, strutting for the girls.

Soon, you begin to get comfortable. You imagine yourself related to this droll old man, dapperly outfitted in a wool jacket, button-down vest, and the traditional Sicilian *coppola* worn by men young and old. You spend hours each day eating, gathered with his huge extended family, enticed by Sicilian dishes—*sfincione*, *caponate*, *carne* by the truckload (one of Nick's second cousins owns a *macelleria*), and an assortment of *dolce* followed by caffè while you listen to *Zio* rattle off jokes with the kind of deadpan delivery stand-up comics kill for.

At the cemetery, where you visit his wife's grave, he gives

you the low-down on the dead.

"You see that grave over there?" He points to a half dozen spectacular sprays of flowers hovering over a freshly dug grave.

"That one wasa killed by the Mafia." He calls your attention to another lavish arrangement of white lilies in the shape of a giant cross.

"Blown up. By the Mafia."

Then he turns somber, motions to a marble mausoleum in pristine condition that looks like Michelangelo might have carved it. Jo curses under his breath, and speaks of the *Cosa Nostra*, which has terrorized his town since he was a boy. He empties out the violets and stale water from the vase that sits in a stand by his wife's grave. Jo is faithful to Lina and brings a fresh bouquet to her site every week but he is bereft without her, and sometimes when he is not nurturing his astounding collection of cacti—hundreds of species that cover his flat rooftop and keep him busy—he wishes for his own death.

Christmas Eve arrives and you're looking forward to a Sicilian Mass but no one is getting dressed. Instead you find yourself playing bingo till 3 a.m., eating homemade honeyed donuts, and laughing out loud at *Zio's* jokes. You don't understand because he is speaking Sicilian, but everyone is in hysterics, especially Aunt Lina's sister Francesca, who must weigh three hundred pounds and is drunk on *Zio's* homemade *grappa*, which tastes like kerosene. You drink, the familial warmth intoxicates, and you feel nested, as though you were born into this family. "*Al mio primo Natale*. To my first Christmas. *Salute!*" you blurt, smiling, the heat of the liquor expanding your lungs. Everyone pantomimes your gesture and drinks to your health. Except Jo, who shifts uncomfortably on his stool.

"You are *Ebrea?*" he asks. You gulp the remaining *grappa* and look to Nick to rescue you from the awkward, *no*, insensitive question, coming from a man who had always felt like a foreigner in the United States, even after receiving his American citizenship. Jo had immigrated to New York just after World War II at the age of forty and worked as a handyman for the Bronx Botanical Gardens long enough to earn a pension before retiring with his wife back to the small town of Lentini, Sicily, where they were born.

"*Si, Zio*, I told you," Nick says. And you let the question slide, because really, maybe, it's a harmless inquiry. Nevertheless— *Ebrea*—that biblical anachronism for Jew, makes you burn, and you flush red, feeling like a relic of ancient Egypt and wonder how in a country with noses like yours you could be outed.

Jo resumes his role as host, but you can't shake your growing discomfort. In Italy, being labeled *Ebrea* feels more offensive than being called *stranieri*, a foreigner—because every non-native is a *straniero*. Even Christiana, your German landlady, married to Marcelo, an Italian, for over twenty years; even Marcelo, who is not a native of the tiny village of San Leo de Batista, where he has lived only *half* his life.

Christmas passes and you begin to feel claustrophobic sleeping in Jo's former bedroom. The bed is too soft, the lighting too dim. Lina's bric-a-brac and perfume bottles clutter the mahogany dresser, still filled with her clothes, while you live out of your suitcase.

Then just before the New Year, Uncle Jo snaps.

"Da tub it isa stopped."

"What?" You and Nick have just come in from a stroll.

"I said de tub. It isa stopped."

"What tub?" you wonder. You only take showers.

"I show you!" he says, exasperated, and marches the two of you upstairs to the bathroom, points first at the toilet, then aims his finger in your direction.

"Deres a shit in da tub and I tink ita was *you!*"

Instantly all the affection you have come to hold for this man disintegrates like ashes at your feet. You feel defiled and small—*una Ebrea*, who despite her best efforts will never be accepted into this tribe. His accusation stings and you sense something underneath this psychotic fit, something that can't be explained or forgiven by age. At that moment he ceases to be *Zio*, and you recall the black and white photos of his four brothers that hang in the sterile, unlived-in living room, the couch and chairs covered for eternity in clear plastic. Jo pointed to Sebastiano, the eldest.

"He was the *Facista* in the family," he remarked grimly.

But now you remember that Jo fought with the Axis in Africa during the War, even though he was conscripted. You think of Nick's father, who also makes you uncomfortable, with his drinking and self-righteousness. Everything around you turns morbid—Sicily, with its Mafia, the old widows, still wearing black twenty years after their husbands' death. Uncle Jo, as frail as he is, becomes a sinister version of himself and you can no more excuse him than you can Mussolini.

In your bedroom that night *you* throw a fit and demand to

leave the next day.

"He had a spell. Don't take it personally," says Nick.

"How should I take it?" you say. "And why didn't you defend me? It wasn't even my shit!"

Nick is laughing. But now you are crying and talking about how it feels to be the only Jewish person in the room, in all of Lentini, in all of Italy, for that matter! You are taking the next train out. Alone, if necessary, you declare.

The following morning, Uncle Jo gets you to the train early. "I'll be back," he says and disappears shrunken behind the wheel of his car. He returns as the train is boarding and contritely offers you a greasy paper bag. Once settled in the compartment, Nick motions you to the open window to wave goodbye.

"*Ciao*, Deb-o-rah," Jo enunciates, giving your name its biblical weight.

"*Ci vediamo*," you say knowing that you will never see him again.

When the train starts moving you open the bag. The *arancini*, named for the orange color of the breadcrumbs clinging to their sides, are still steaming. You take one out in its greasy wax paper wrapping and bite into its center. The texture is crispy and creamy, a nutritious, hearty meal filled with the simple foods upon which this civilization is built. But it's more than just food. It's an apology, and the remorse you feel makes you savor it even more. Years later, you will discover *Mozzicato*, an Italian bakery in Hartford that makes these Sicilian treats, but they will never taste the same.

CATFISH

by Brianna Goldberg

ITS slippery whiskers, spine, and fins curl around the wide, red pot. An entire catfish, hefty and brown, all of its curves in a perfect *C*.

A terrible surprise. And I hate myself for thinking that. *You sissy, you closed-minded jerk.*

I squeeze the lid handle. I'm stuck, wincing at a stew whose main ingredient's eyes are glaring, moustache waving, down inside the broth. I don't know whether to cover the pot, so I won't have to see it anymore, or to keep the lid off and look.

We asked Esther to cook us Nigerian dishes half the days of the week because we wanted to learn about local food. We'd tried a bit already. Sometimes, for lunch, the office assistant would bring in stacks of Tupperware filled with steaming food—musky stews, or steaming cassava cooked since early morning by a "mama" whose propane stove smoked dirtily in the ditch at the side of the road.

"Wow," the assistant would say, as I closed my eyes and opened my mouth. In the food would go, the flavours in shocking mixes like dreams where people from different areas of your life interact seamlessly as part of the same world.

I'd chomp hard into a bay leaf hidden in the grit of bitter greens; taste smoked fish and chunks of spicy beef slicked with orangey-red palm oil; mop up the juice in the corner with a dob of fermented dough pinched between my fingers. I'd eat until I got to the bottom of the container, just to show him I wasn't afraid, my belly dense like a cannonball.

"Wow," he'd say. "Do you *really* like it?"

But that was just a "sometimes" lunch. The idea of regular Nigerian-style home cooking was even more appealing, interesting, provocative. What would we be eating if we were actually from here? If Esther were our family rather than our housekeeper? We didn't want to be those shitty expats who move to some far-away country only to spend the whole time at a restaurant serving shitty expat fare. Those shitty expats who come into a place, tell people what to do based on expat cultural beliefs, and then peace out, leaving locals to clean up the mess. We wanted to be in it, learn from it, *taste it.*

But when I asked Esther if she'd like to cook for us a few nights a week, her eyes popped wide.

"Really? Why?"

I explained: the local food experience. And besides, her one-year-old, Happiness—wrapped on her back with colourful fabric that you might think was African but actually came from the Netherlands, via China, to be sold in the local market—had been sick recently, and she'd mentioned their family could use a bit more cash.

"Okayyyyy!" She laughed in a nervous way, agreeing.

Saint she is, Esther started us in easy: a greens-filled soup, spicy tomato-paste rice and string beans, chunks of goat or beef or sometimes chicken.

Now, in the kitchen, here was the catfish. Staring, threatening, defiant. *How do you like Nigerian food now*, it seemed to say.

I'd eaten the fish before, but it had been disguised. In the park where the bombs went off, that's where we'd often go for catfish and beer.

One of my first weekends in Abuja, a co-worker drove us up to the fish park, its central tiled building glowing blue-white with floodlights in the night. Patio furniture jumbled around it in the biggest, widest dark. We sat in the shadows.

"They've started putting in better lighting since the bombs," my co-worker told me. Oh good.

That first time in the park, I braced through every microsecond, planning what I would do if another bomb were to explode: maybe take cover in the toilet shed or run out to the main street… unless, of course, the explosion were to happen closer, and by the time you would have realized it, you would have been missing a limb or half your face, or been reduced to droplets of former person.

By the time *I* would have realized it. By the time *I* would have been missing a limb, or been reduced to droplets of former person. Fun.

There were many nights in the fish park after that. It's where we'd go to relax after work, to celebrate special dinners, to linger with Sunday night beers after playing sports on the unkempt elementary school field. That was how things were done, so that was how we'd do it.

Sitting on cracked white plastic chairs, we'd order "fish and chips." It would take a really long time for the food to arrive. I'd see the young men down in the charcoal pit diligently turning cricket-paddle-sized river fish wrapped in aluminum, but the cooking was slow.

We'd drink extra large bottles of beer that tasted like chemicals. We'd feel rats scurrying underfoot. We'd talk louder during the nearby call to prayer as bats circled the minarets. I kept spraying myself with insect repellent because I had stopped taking anti-malarials—they made me feel unsteady. We'd chat and laugh and I'd wonder, "Is anybody having a good time? Is anybody else thinking about the bombs? Would they sound like a pop or a bang?"

Then much, much later, a young man would set down a platter and someone would unfoil the giant roasted catfish, the whole thing, soggy French fries stuffed under its belly and all along its sides with onions and ass-burningly spicy peppers. Everyone would dig at it, bare handed, in the darkness, ripping hunks of flesh off the skeleton. I would dive in to show how cool I was, how open to trying everything. I hated the spongy, slimy fish but loved the burning peppers and chips, so perfect against the beer and the deep night and the bug spray.

One of these fish park nights was a going-away dinner for an office assistant. Our boss cleared his throat and launched into a speech, grandly wishing the assistant well. The person next to him toasted. Around the table, it was coming to me, a chain of inside jokes, anecdotes.

The assistant leaving was the first creative person I met in Nigeria, a young poet; I'd cared about him fiercely right away. We traded poems, writing. And he insisted on coming with me when I wanted to report on a political demonstration, he wanted to help and protect me. We left the scene when anti-terror police showed up with bomb-sniffing dogs, telling the crowd there'd been an explosives threat. He and I got into a car with a local BBC stringer who drove us back to our office. I didn't know him, but I got in the car. It all felt like a weird dream.

The farewell speeches came round the table at me. The catfish was picked clean. I thought about that story of the bomb threat. How could I turn any of it into a light-hearted toast?

Find the humour in the fear, find the balance, I thought. *Everyone who's "from here" is doing it, just do like them.* I gulped a breath and my voice caught with crying. I don't know if they could see.

In the kitchen now, though, it's just the fish and me. I can throw it out, but then I'll have to carry it down the block to the dumpster. If I don't, Esther will find it in the bin when she cleans up tomorrow, and I don't want to offend her. If I do, the barefoot security boys at our gate will notice me throwing something out, mention it to Esther as a joke, and she'll figure it out anyway. I suppose I could break it up really small, to flush down the toilet.

No. I will not be that person. I will not be afraid.

I ladle the juice and the vegetables into a shallow bowl, press the spoon edge against catfish back to break off a piece of meat. The skin doesn't give, though—it is strong. Eyes are staring, whiskers fluttering like one of those goofy five-fingered goodbye waves. I reach for the serrated bread knife and hack into the fish's face. I want to cut it off like the head of a snake. Hack, hack, hack. But it's a helmet of heavy bone. Now there are shards of meat and skin all around its neck. I keep feeling the resistance of knife hitting skull even after I stop trying. A sense memory I can't shake.

I want to give up, but close my eyes, gather my will and change tactics, slicing a hunk of side meat still attached to the floppy, slippy skin, and covering the pot.

Perching on the edge of the couch, I balance the bowl on my lap.

The stew is lukewarm because Esther cooked it earlier this afternoon when she came in to clean the apartment—not at our request, but because this is all part of the deal of living here. I like to clean my own house. I like to cook my own food. But this is how it's done here, so this is how we do it. And besides, Esther needs the money for her family.

A cool mouthful of catfish slides off the spoon, into my mouth, and I crunch down through what must be seventy trillion tiny fish bones. My friend told me the thing to do is just to eat them, really chew them up. *They're good for you,* she said. *This is how we do it.*

But I can't help it. I use my tongue to separate the flesh. On the lip of the bowl, I spit out the bones.

DISCOMFORT FOOD

by Maggie Downs

MY mother was a lot of things, but a good cook wasn't one of them. She boiled the color out of vegetables and cooked noodles until they dissolved. All protein, from fish to fowl, was dredged in all-purpose flour, then fried in a skillet with a sprinkle of dried parsley. No salt. No pepper. No flavor.

Once, when I was in high school and having dinner at a friend's house, I had to ask what I was eating.

"It's chicken," my friend's mother said, and I was shocked. I had no idea chicken could be moist.

No doubt my mom would have resented the food that filled her kitchen after her death. She would have thought everyone was showing off, especially when it came to the tiny finger sandwiches from the ladies' guild at her church and the potato salad decorated with radish roses. Oh, she would have hated that.

She also would have been sad to see other people offering sustenance to my siblings and me. Our mom grew up during World War II, a childhood spent with an aching, empty belly, and she wanted more for her children. So while she didn't always give us the proper food to fill our bodies—Hostess cupcakes and Tab, iceberg lettuce and broccoli cooked until it turned grey—she made certain we were never hungry. She loved us to the point of fattening us up.

• • •

My mom had only been dead for one day when the casseroles arrived.

First was a turkey dumpling bake from the next-door neighbor. They threw in a cherry cheesecake for good measure. The people across the street carried over Southwest Tamale Pie, a layered dish of chicken, tortillas, cheddar cheese, and Ro-Tel canned tomatoes. A Post-it note gave stern reheating instructions ("Do NOT remove from oven until brown and bubbly").

My dad's old friend brought lasagna—two kinds, meat and vegetable—plus a punch bowl filled to the brim with iceberg lettuce and homemade ranch dressing. "You need to watch out for your own health," he said when he handed it over.

My sister's hairdresser gave us a square pan of slippery beef noodles with mushrooms. Her workout partner whipped up her specialty, Cowboy Casserole, a hearty mix of ground beef, chili beans, tater tots and cream cheese. For the vegetarians, a teacher from the local elementary school gave us a small container of

Broccoli Salad Surprise. The surprise was that it contained bacon.

My mother's death was the first in my immediate family, so I was shocked by the volume and array of food—the nonstop deliveries, the loaves of bread that seemed like Jesus himself multiplied them for the masses.

During those somber days, my newly abbreviated family ended up with enough food to feed us for months. This is how people mourn in the Midwestern town where I grew up. Here the grieving process was constructed out of casserole dishes, and sympathy was baked into nine-by-thirteen-inch rectangles.

When the fridge overflowed with foil-wrapped pans, our freezer carried the rest of the burden. The kitchen counter was stacked with additional, equally practical gifts. Paper plates, plastic cutlery, napkins and Kleenex. Temporary things, things that could be discarded.

Our neighbors had obviously done this before. Each pan was marked with a streak of masking tape, the owner's name handwritten across it with Sharpie. We were allowed to be sad, sure. But we still had to return the cookware.

• • •

My mom spent a decade dying of Alzheimer's disease, gradually becoming a husk of a woman. First she forgot my name, then she forgot how to speak, and finally she forgot how to walk. That's the thing about Alzheimer's—it's not only that the mind abandons the person with the disease. It's that the mind completely disconnects from everything else. It's like tugging all the hoses and wires from under a car's hood and expecting the vehicle to still run. It won't.

When she lost the ability to eat and swallow, my mom was moved from a nursing home to hospice. My family had decided a long time ago that we wouldn't put my mother on a feeding tube, so once she moved to hospice, we knew it was only a matter of time before she succumbed to insufficient nutrition.

My mom, who spent her adult life counting calories, watching her figure, and sampling every fad diet, starved to death in just a few days.

• • •

When I peeked into her open casket, I didn't expect her to look so beautiful, so much like the mom I once knew. Her cheeks bloomed like carnations. Her blonde hair was teased and sprayed into a halo of perfect curls. She wore her prettiest blue dress, a dress she hadn't worn in ages, even long before the Alzheimer's, because of a few stubborn pounds.

I remembered when I was a little girl, maybe six or seven years old, and my mom introduced me to the concept of a weekly weigh-in. First she stepped on the scale, then she recorded the number on a handmade chart that was taped to the back of the bathroom door. Then it was my turn. I stepped on the scale, put my hands on my hips, and moaned in a perfect imitation of my mom. "Fifty-six pounds?" I'd cry out. "I'm disgusting."

I wished I could gather up all that weight now, all those pounds gained and shed, and give them back to her. I'd use those calories to nourish her for one more day. One more hour. I wondered what happened to the weight that she lost. Where were those pieces of my mother now?

In her coffin, she looked so real and ripe. I could almost imagine curling up beside her. I touched her hand to be sure she was dead. Her skin was cold, and I pulled back with surprise.

I didn't realize I was shaking until my aunt put an arm around my shoulders and led me into the funeral home kitchen. She pointed to a plastic sleeve of wheat bread and a platter of cold cuts.

"Let me make you a sandwich," my aunt said. "We've got that spicy mustard you like."

In the deepest throes of grief, I didn't actively eat as much as I allowed myself to be fed.

• • •

My mom was buried on a gentle slope in a veterans' cemetery in Dayton, Ohio, the place where my retired Air Force dad will someday join her. The cemetery staff plowed through the snow to make room for our cars. They rolled out fake grass where my mom's coffin rested during the brief service. There was a small shelter, but the wind was punishing, and I howled in pain. I had never felt so cold.

During the sad, angry days that followed, my brother

polished off a chocolate cake, while my sister dipped ridged potato chips into bowls of fluffy mashed potatoes and fed them to me.

"If only we could add another form of potato to this," I said. "Then I'd be happy."

But the truth was that I could not eat enough comfort food to feel comforted.

With all the dishes that were generously cooked and brought to my home, nothing could satisfy what I felt—a wild, heavy hunger, almost as powerful as what my mother felt as her body betrayed her—and nothing ever would.

Our mother was German. She came from the land that coined the term *kummerspeck* or "grief bacon"—excess weight gained from emotional overeating. As her offspring, we understood that concept so well, this eating to fill all the empty spaces.

Our neighbors instinctively knew it too, which explained all the noodles, cakes and salad, the freezer full of casseroles, and the counter full of bread. They simply wanted us to be full again.

MESSY

by Teri Vlassopoulos

BEFORE getting pregnant I'd looked forward to cravings. What kind of bizarre combinations of food would my body ask for in the middle of the night? I imagined pregnancy would have a similar effect to the miracle berries I'd read about in Adam Leith Gollner's *The Fruit Hunters*—a berry that alters your perception of the food you're eating, making lemons and vinegar sugary sweet. A few weeks into my pregnancy I sat down for dinner, took a forkful of chicken and realized that it didn't taste right. Was it too dry? I took another experimental bite, but couldn't muster the energy to keep eating and pushed it away. And then at breakfast, the thought of eggs—runny-yolked, soft, my favourite—made my stomach turn. I went out for Korean barbecue and the bowls of red raw meat waiting to be cooked on the grills in front of us were even more unappealing. Better a bowl of vegetarian bibimbap, hold the yolky egg, but without it to swirl around and bind the rice to the hot stone bowl, the meal was lackluster. Dejected, I realized that instead of cravings, I'd developed aversions.

In those early weeks of pregnancy it was a struggle to figure out which foods I could eat. Peanut butter toast, grilled cheese sandwiches and cereal were fine. While regular, honestly cooked chicken was off limits, McDonald's Junior Chicken sandwiches provided a modicum of protein. Bananas were safe until I ate one and then immediately threw up in the closest public bathroom; the association lingered. It was a relief, then, when one by one foods regained their appeal and in celebration I made myself a solo dinner of soft scrambled eggs. I kept my hopes up for cravings, but they never quite materialized, and although there were some satisfying drive-out-of-my-way chocolate milkshakes and 3:00 a.m. peanut butter sandwiches, nothing tasted as transcendent as I'd hoped. But as the weeks ticked by I learned that my pregnancy, like most pregnancies, wasn't going to unfold exactly according to a textbook and that the best course of action would be to just deal with things as they happened rather than anticipate them.

Though sometimes things were predictable. In my last month I was overcome with a maniacal desire to clean. Nesting, it turns out, is a real, intense urge. So I cleaned and I organized, and it seemed better to avoid cooking because of the traces it would leave behind—splotches on the now sparkling stovetop, crumbs on the counter, bowls and pots in the sink requiring another do-over. After I rearranged the cutlery tray and the pantry, they were simply too orderly, too neat to rifle through again. I knew that once the baby was born this level of cleanliness would be impossible to maintain, and that is probably the point of nesting: it's one last chance of having absolute control over your environment, of getting things *just right* before they slowly, imperceptibly, spiraled away. It was maybe an exaggeration, but at the time, the baby's imminent birth felt like an absolute deadline, the delineation between life switching from clean to messy, easy to hard. Either way, not cooking made sense—as my due date approached, people told my husband and me to take advantage of our free nights to eat out.

Go to restaurants, go to the movies, go on vacation. This was the advice given to us most frequently, as if none of these things would be possible post-baby. Rather than question it, we followed the advice gladly. For vacation we went to Charleston, South Carolina in September. We'd passed through the city years ago on a road trip and had always wanted to return, partially for the food (fluffy biscuits, sausage gravy, grits, seafood), partially for the beaches, which would still be welcoming at the tail end of summer. By the time we left for Charleston, I felt like I'd hit my stride in my pregnancy too. I was eating normally and I didn't feel exhausted all the time. I hadn't thrown up in weeks. At the last ultrasound we'd seen the baby in my belly, her round head, her spindly body, and felt reassured. So Charleston was a welcome break: we slept in, we went to those beaches, we ate out.

While the restaurant meals were all wonderful, the one I keep returning to wasn't actually in a restaurant. We'd driven to Savannah for a day trip, but before heading back to Charleston we stopped at a seafood shop to pick up something to eat. We hadn't had a Low Country Boil yet, one of South Carolina's well-known seafood dishes, and we'd heard that this shop did a good one. After a short wait the man at the counter handed over a sealed aluminum tray. It looked like a reasonable size until I held it and felt the heft of what was inside: a few pounds of shrimp, crab, sausage, corn and potatoes that had been seasoned and boiled together in one pot. It was too much food for only two of us, but what could we do other than put the tray in the car and drive somewhere to eat it? We went to Tybee Beach, which I remembered as being busy, a little touristy, but since it was now late afternoon and mid-September, the sprawling beach was mostly empty. We laid out the sheet we'd bought from Family Dollar as our picnic blanket, opened up the aluminum tray and started eating. It was all very messy—peeling slippery shrimp, wrestling crab legs. Plastic cutlery wasn't much use so we used our hands and because we were concentrating too hard on making a dent into the pile of food we didn't speak much.

A few days earlier we'd bought a watermelon from a farm stand, but kept forgetting it in the rental car. It was on the backseat floor and whenever one of us would step too hard on the brake, the sound of it rolling around would alert us to its existence. It got riper and riper in the sun-warmed car until I finally remembered it that day at Tybee Beach. After my fill of the boil, I cut into the watermelon for dessert. It leaked a blood-red sweet syrup onto the sheet, and then, when we ate slices of it, onto our clothes, down our arms and chins.

When we were finally finished we threw out the remains— the shells, the food we simply couldn't eat, the watermelon rinds. Seagulls shrieked in the distance and slowly circled the garbage bins. They knew it was their turn. Because we hadn't brought enough napkins, we were a mess, but it was still warm out and the sun was bright, so we put on our bathing suits and went swimming in high tide. The water washed away the dinner stickiness and replaced it with ocean saltiness instead. Every so often a silvery fish would leap up out of the waves right in front of us. Pelicans flew low to the water as well, tracking those fish for their own dinner. Afterward we sat on the sheet until we dried off. We shook the sand off our feet before putting on our shoes, but it was impossible to get rid of all of it so I felt the grittiness against my soles as we walked to the car and then drove back to Charleston at dusk.

I thought of this meal during my nesting phase precisely because it had been such a sloppy one. I was compelled to clean, yes, but I reminded myself that it wasn't such a big deal if I didn't have the time to be so detailed later. I'd reassured myself many times throughout my pregnancy that it was okay if things weren't textbook perfect, if I didn't experience everything I thought I would or if something unexpected popped up—we would just deal with it, forge on. It would be the same after the baby came, I told myself, even more so since surely unpredictability would be a daily occurrence. But like that meal at the beach in South Carolina, it was often the messy things that I remembered more vividly, after all. The ad hoc cleanup done afterward was not always efficient, but it could still be good enough, and maybe even more than that, better than that. Maybe even kind of perfect.

FEED THE BIRDS

by Vivek Shraya

THE most creative school lunches were made after my parents purchased a sandwich maker. One of my mom's co-workers had raved about hers, and my mom took her coworkers' raves very seriously. The convenience of the sandwich maker only further confirmed her faith. Preparing lunch for me and my brother became so much easier with a machine. Two slices of bread, ketchup, mustard, and butter smashed together with a surprise filling. One week it was frozen hash browns, the next week it was falafel, another it was just sliced cheese.

The sandwich was complemented by a morning snack, fruit, and a juicebox. The morning snack was either crackers packaged with a rectangular red stick and processed cheese spread or the classic granola bar, and the fruit was either an apple or an orange.

I am not an orange person.

Oranges are an impractical and exasperating food. The first peel is the greatest challenge. Getting in far enough to reach the top layer of the fruit but not accidentally thumbing into the fruit itself and getting juice sprayed in the eye. Or not peeling in far enough and being stuck working against the defensive white rind. Then there is the work of the peeling itself. When you finally get to eat the fruit, you end up biting seeds. Who doesn't love a crunchy fruit? And just so that you don't forget all that you've endured, there is that orange smell that refuses to leave your hands. You will smell orange for the rest of the day—as you type, when you scratch your face, even after you wash your hands with soap. This is a reminder that in the battle of Orange vs. Human, you may have trespassed through the peel, secured the fruit, and even found a way to ignore the annoyance of spitting out seeds in the midst of your citrus pleasure—but the orange, by marking you with its odour, always emerges victorious.

And what can I say about granola bars? As an adult, it is no surprise to me that the word granola has now become synonymous for *boring* or *bland*. Even the premium granola bars—chocolate chip—made me wish for chocolate chips on their own.

Around Grade 8, I decided that I had had my fill of oranges and granola bars. But I couldn't bring myself to throw them out in the giant metal garbage bins that lined our school hallways. I had been taught at Sunday school that *Food is God*. How could I throw God out?

It was perhaps Sunday school that also provided the sacred solution: *why throw God out when I could feed the birds?* The food wouldn't be wasted and I could feel good about my humanitarian efforts (another Sunday school teaching: *Love All Serve All*).

I began stockpiling the oranges and granola bars in brown paper lunch bags under the stack of audaciously patterned sweaters I had borrowed from my dad. After a month or two, when the sweaters could no longer efficiently conceal the bumpy shapes the stacked food made, I carried stuffed bags of now moldy oranges and granola bars to the field in between my school and my home and left them as an offering to the (presumably hungry) winged creatures of the sky.

Occasionally, I felt guilty about my moldy offerings, worrying that perhaps I was poisoning the birds. But I told myself that birds likely picked around the mold. That's what beaks were for! Besides—mold probably didn't affect birds the way it affected humans.

One spring, I had a particularly large stock and had to make two deposits. The snow had started to melt and create shallow ponds. I dropped my first bag of food into one of these ponds. If the birds didn't find the food in the water, perhaps other wildlife would. Either way, I was comforted knowing the food wouldn't be wasted.

As I left my house for the second time that afternoon, carrying my second offering, my mother's grey Topaz pulled up into the driveway. I hurried back into the house and reburied the food in my closet.

"How was your day?" she asked.

(harmless question stay calm)

"It was good, Mom!"

(it was a good day this isn't a lie I have nothing to hide)

"What were you doing just now?"

(oh God she knows she knows she knows she knows she knows)

"Me?"

(oh God why is she looking at me I hate when she looks at me when she knows)

"Yes, you."

(you are such a bad liar she knows she knows she knows)

"Nothing much."

(you are SUCH a bad liar she knows she knows she knows)

"You looked like you were up to something…"

(how does she always know just don't look at her don't say anything)

"You had something in your hand," she continued, "something brown… where were you going?"

(how did she see that from her car how does she see everything she knows don't say it don't say it)

"Oh. Um. I was going to feed the birds."

I said it. There was no other way this could play out. I had never been good at lying, especially not to my mother. I adored her, but I was terrified of her too. Her parenting style was fierce—both in the way she loved and in her punishments. I also believed she might be moved by my well-intentioned efforts to give back to the planet.

So when she asked, "What do you mean, you feed the birds?" I told her everything—about the moldy oranges and the granola bars in my closet, how I didn't like them, and how I thought the birds could benefit from my dislike.

She listened and then asked me to bring to the kitchen the food that was left in my closet. While I was gone, my dad came home and I heard her filling him in in an even tone. That's when I began to worry. The disappearance of melody from her tone never boded well.

"Can you show your dad where you left the food for the birds?" she asked, when I came back into the kitchen. "And bring the food home."

"But," I said, "it will be wet from the pond."

"That's ok. Just bring it home." Then she turned to my dad. "Make sure he brings all of it home," she said, as though she hadn't just instructed me to do the same.

My dad and I walked in silence. This wasn't unusual, but this time the silence felt deliberate on his part and I was grateful.

When we got to the field, I pointed to the bag.

"There it is."

He nodded.

I reached into the cold, brown water and pulled out the full bag.

"Is there anything else?" He questioned the water, ignoring my *No.* When he seemed satisfied by not being able to see any more food himself, we walked home. Again, in silence.

"Did you get it?" my mother asked when we returned.

"Yes," we answered in unison.

My mom was sitting at her usual chair at the dinner table. The oranges and granola bars from my closet were now laid out on my placemat. She took the wet bag from my hand and laid the soaking contents next to the dry ones.

"Sit down," she directed. Even tone.

I sat and waited for a lecture. It never came.

"Now. Eat."

I looked up at her.

"But…"

"Eat."

"…the mold?"

"Yes."

"But…"

"Eat."

With the repetition of that one word, she conveyed the futility of protesting. I knew I could say anything at this point (*I have to go to the bathroom… I was trying to help the environment… What if I get sick?*) and her response would be a single word: *Eat.* I started with the dry granola bars. *Maybe these weren't so bad after all,* I thought, prompted by the sight of a dozen moldy oranges waiting to be consumed. Then I moved to the wet granola bars, which were only slightly more moist than usual inside the drenched wrapping. My mother continued to sit with me, watching me eat. My dad washed the dishes.

Eventually, it was the dreaded orange time. I began to peel, knowing that these oranges, largely covered in creamy white and blue bruises, would have to enter my mouth, be tasted by my tongue, and pass down my throat.

"Can I have some water?" I had been known to swallow whole other foods I didn't enjoy at dinner (onions, beet roots, cabbage), forcing them down with large gulps of water. It had become a running joke even—*There he goes again… swallowing…*

Not this time.

What I remember after this is the gagging. Gagging and more gagging. My mom watching me gag. Me gagging more. And then, strangely, being grateful. Being grateful for my body's own water, saliva, which helped me swallow. Being grateful that those awful orange peels were surprisingly water resistant. Being grateful when twelve moldy oranges became eleven, then ten, and eventually zero.

My mother stood up.

"Your dad works hard," she said. "Every day. To feed you. And this is what you do?"

"But Mom, you pack the same thing every day," I said, quietly.

"So? It's what we can afford."

Since that day, my family and I have never discussed me throwing out food, nor my mother's response, though occasionally a joke is made about how I used to like to feed the birds. She seemed confident her punishment would ensure that I never threw food out again, and I now had a new story in my arsenal of *Crazy Mom Stories* to share with friends. Looking back, understanding now just how hard my immigrant parents did work, how much they did to provide for me and my brother (my mom worked a full-time job and went to school part-time), I almost feel as though her punishment wasn't severe enough.

The next day at school, when I opened my lunch bag and found the predictable, yet purposed, granola bar and orange, I thought of my mother's face and of mold and gagged, remembering the lesson I had learned only twelve hours earlier.

Then I threw the granola bar and orange into the garbage.

FAT FREE

by Jane Campbell

WHEN I was four years old, my mother brought me to a dim office tucked away in the far corner of a sprawling hospital complex. I remember brown. Brown walls. Brown filing cabinet. Brown sofa. The office smelled like band-aids. I had to sit in a grown up chair. My feet swung inches above the floor. My heels smacked against the chair legs.

We were in a nutritionist's office, and I was about to embark on my very first diet.

The nutritionist was neither beautiful nor threatening. When I think of the day now, I see in her in a white lab coat. She has long, blonde hair. It's dyed. Her highlights are cheap and chunky. But I can't really remember this. I must have cross-referenced her with some other figure from my murky, early past. Someone else I didn't like. In any case, this is the image I have of her: blonde hair, manicured fingernails that clicked across the desk, falsely cheery.

Up until that point, I had never given any thought at all to what I ate or to whether or not it was "healthy." I probably knew how much I weighed, because I liked to know facts about myself, but I didn't know what it meant to be overweight. My body was just my body. It was just there. I had never thought of myself as beautiful or ugly, fat or thin.

Over the course of our meeting with the nutritionist, I gained a whole new perspective. I weighed too much. I ate too much. My body was not a natural, inert thing. It was something I had to control. It was a problem I needed to fix.

The nutritionist told my mother and me that if I got hungry between meals I should snack on carrots or celery dipped in fat-free ranch dressing. She added that her own daughter ate this every day when she got home from school.

• • •

The next time my mother went to the grocery store, she brought me baby carrots and fat-free Hidden Valley ranch. In the afternoons, I sat cross-legged in front of the coffee table in our living room and carefully rolled each carrot in the viscous, paper-white dressing. It tasted sweet in an unappealing, vaguely chemical way.

I ate my carrots slowly, deliberately. One at a time. When the last carrot was gone, I wanted absolutely nothing more than to eat another.

• • •

So how fat was I when I started dieting? How fat can a four-year-old possibly be? I've forgotten exactly how much I weighed. My pediatric growth charts are lost to history. The only evidence I have is photographic. It sits in an old Nike box underneath my desk. "Jane—photos" is written on the side in permanent marker. My mother's handwriting.

Four years old. Marigold hair. Pouting at the breakfast table. Sitting at her father's desk with a ballpoint pen in hand, wearing a serious expression. Earnestly shushing her fussing baby brother. Running into the ocean's cold froth, fearless, no hesitation. All these memories I don't remember. A face that's familiar but not exactly my own.

So how fat was I? I wasn't fat at all.

I was maybe a little bit chubby. But only in the way young children often are. I look well fed, well cared-for, loved. I was baby-fat, not fat-fat. One growth spurt away from being thin.

By the time I was seven or eight, I'd developed a routine. Every morning, I woke up and promised myself I would be good. I would eat only half my school lunch. I would have carrot sticks and ranch dressing when I got home from school. I would not snack before dinner. I would not finish my dinner. I would not snack after dinner. I would go to bed hungry. I would wake up again and repeat the process.

Every day, I failed. Most days I didn't even make it 'til dinnertime. I ate a classmate's birthday cupcake. My friend's mother bought me ice cream. We were out of baby carrots so I had cheese and crackers instead. I wandered into the kitchen and got a cookie out of the snack drawer without even really thinking about it. Almost like I was sleepwalking.

Every day, somehow, I fucked up. I ate the wrong foods. I ate too much. I figured, Well I've blown it for today, so I might as well eat what I want. Tomorrow, I'll be perfect and then I'll be perfect every day for the rest of my life. I'll never eat cookies or cheese or more than exactly one half-cup of vanilla frozen yogurt ever again for the rest of my life. For the rest of my life I'll be good. For the rest of my life I'll be hungry—so today, I might as well eat.

This is how I spent most nights when I was a child— slipping in and out of the kitchen like a tiny pickpocket. I'd stand in the refrigerator door and shovel leftovers into my mouth with my hands. I'd grab a handful of cookies and eat them quickly, with purpose, hunched over the open snack drawer. I only ate when I was alone, when my mother was out or distracted or in another part of the house. I listened for footsteps in the hallway and I always kept one eye on the door so I could make a quick escape.

I still got caught. Often. Sometimes my mother said nothing. She just let her eyebrows drop, a sharp, unmistakable look of disappointment. Sometimes she shook her head. Sometimes she got angry. *Are you sure you want to eat that? I just bought this, how does it not fit? Why are you still eating? Why don't you just stop eating!*

I didn't want to be fat, but as much as I tried I couldn't change it. I started to feel like my mother didn't just want me to be skinny; she wanted me to be a totally different person.

• • •

When I was twenty-seven years old, newly married, at a "normal" weight after a final, finally successful diet in my early twenties, I bought a bottle of fat free ranch on sale at No Frills. I hadn't eaten it in years. I thought, *Maybe it's better than I remember?*

It wasn't. I tried it. My husband tried it. "This tastes so bad, it actually depresses me," he said. I agreed. I threw the bottle in the trash, still full. I didn't bother cleaning it out for recycling and I'm usually good about that.

At first, this was where I planned to end the story: girl gets married, girl rids herself of fat-free ranch, girl rides off into the sunset. But that's not really how it ends. Not when I still spend money I don't have on spin classes, still feel a wave of panic when my jeans start to feel a little tight, still scan nutrition facts and keep a scale at the foot of my bed. Not when there are still three bags of baby carrots sitting in my fridge.

• • •

I know it's unfair to blame my mother. She thought she was helping me. She thought we'd go to the nutritionist, I'd learn about healthy eating, my weight would drop into the normal range on the growth charts, and then I'd grow up and forget. If only time worked differently. If only she could have looked into the future and seen me at fourteen, bent over a trashcan, my finger down my throat. If she could have seen me at seventeen, drunk, skirt hiked up in a stairwell, straddling a guy I barely knew, just for the sake of feeling wanted. If she could have seen me at twenty-two, when I weighed

240 pounds, when I dreaded leaving the house, and ate alone, in bed, late at night, when I could be sure no one was watching. If only. Maybe. What if. Might have been.

This is the great tragedy of raising a child: you don't get to choose the memories that stick. All those nights your daughter curled into your chest, the long drives when you laughed until your teeth hurt, the picking of flowers in the fragrant heat of late summer, toes curled into the soil. These memories are dull for her. Half-remembered dreams. But she can still hear her feet smack into the chair at the nutritionist's office. She can still see you standing in the kitchen, an empty cracker box in your hand. "Did really you eat this whole thing? Really? That's disgusting." Those are the words she remembers verbatim, while so much tenderness is lost.

• • •

It's true, now, that I'm better than I was. I'm done trying to lose those last twenty pounds. I don't throw up or starve myself. I will never fall for another fad diet. But I can't deny that some part of me is still waiting to become the girl my mother wanted, the girl she probably wanted to become herself. The girl who eats carrots and fat-free ranch every day, who sits down for her precise, healthy snack, and then clears the table, puts the food away. I'm still waiting to become the girl who can say that's enough, who doesn't want seconds, who finally feels full.

POMEGRANATES

by Lauren Razavi

AS I walk through the restaurant door, I am overwhelmed by the sensations of home. I have never been to Iran, but my memories of growing up have a distinct Iranian flavour. I greet the waiter in broken Farsi and ask for a table. The taste of the foreign words on my tongue is addictive; I don't get the chance to use them very often. With me are my boyfriend and his friends, another couple. I've dragged us all the way across London, from Embankment to Shepherd's Bush, to spend the evening at a Persian restaurant. I'm fidgety with excitement, like a kid at a birthday party.

A trio of Iranian gents one table over playfully demands to know where we're going when we step outside for a smoke. The men have pregnant-round bellies and tuck their napkins into their collars. They're well-dressed and a little beyond middle age, the way I'm used to seeing Iranian men. They ask if the food's that bad and then shout across the room to the owner—a friend, it seems—who rolls his eyes in a way I imagine means, "Screw you, you old jokers."

When the food arrives, our new friends want to know what we think of it. The question, again, sounds like a demand. Most things Iranians say sound like demands.

After I excuse myself to the bathroom, a familiar smell hits me as I descend a black spiral staircase to the basement. The scent is strong enough to throw me back a decade or two. It's the fragrance of a Persian kitchen at rest. Just a whiff tells me the dish that's been simmering there all day. My mind conjures the image of fluffy Persian rice, garnished with strands of saffron and huge dollops of butter, and a meaty stew full of fresh herbs and fat butter beans. *Ghormeh sabzi*. It's the kind of dish that a Persian won't serve up unless it's been stewing over a flame for hours.

I'd like to be able to say that Iranians, and their cuisine in Iran, are the same as all this, that this is an accurate portrayal of the country, casually dropped into a West London restaurant. But the truth is I don't know. My understanding of Iran, its culture and its people, is made up only of my experiences in the expat community—and most Iranian expats I've met left their country twenty or thirty years ago. I ache to know this place, Iran, and for my ponderings and observations to be made up of more substance than a night like this.

• • •

"You're doing it wrong."

At fourteen years old, hearing these words from my father— whatever the reason for them—has a tendency to cause tears. It's a stage of life where I'm constantly temperamental, and Dad and I struggle to negotiate each other.

My primary concerns at this time are music, boys and friends—in that order. I'm an only child, and my dad has limited experience in dealing with Western teenage girls. It's the weekend, and he has, daringly, decided to embark on a cooking lesson with me.

I don't cry this time, though. I'm focused on the task at hand, because it's at this age I've begun flirting with my Persian heritage as a fascinating sideline to the everyday. Moments of insight into my father's life before my birth are rare, and I've already learned to appreciate them. He doesn't like to talk about the past, about his upbringing or what he remembers of Iran. But food is the thing that always prompts those rare conversations. His memories of food are the ones he deems safe, the ones he doesn't mind sharing with his teenage daughter.

"You have to cut off the stems just where they begin," he says, elbowing me out of the way to chop the spring onions himself. "Otherwise, you end up with stringy bits in the stew."

It occurs to me that there are worse things than having stringy bits in *ghormeh sabzi*. Then I realize that I've never found any stringy bits in any Persian dish I've ever eaten. It's in that realization that my understanding of Persian food truly begins.

• • •

In all the places I've visited during my years of travelling the world as a writer—from the tourist hot-spots to the borrowed countryside homes—I have never found another culture that takes quite as much pride in its food as the Persian one does. Choosing the right produce, sinking into the rituals of preparation, decorating the family table and, finally, serving a gargantuan meal with dazzling hospitality; these are time-honoured Iranian specialities. Every dish is a celebration of the country's rich history and culture. Every breakfast, lunch, and dinner is a painstakingly wrought ceremony, allowed to be nothing less than perfect. A place's food can evoke the symptoms of its culture—and this is especially true of Iran.

Iranians are hospitable guests and remarkable hosts, and such reputations are not a matter of class. The poorest families in the slums of Tehran and Mashhad fall over themselves to serve their best meal on their finest crockery, even for an uninvited guest. This is part of the bend-over-backwards form of hospitality called *tarof*, a tradition that is followed without question by those raised in an Iranian environment. It's so ingrained that it took me until my twenties to learn there was a dedicated word for it.

Tarof requires a special brand of attentiveness and observation. Accurate judgments of a person's reaction to a situation are crucial. When I was young, my Iranian cousins and I, although all raised in the West, joked about the secret formula of how much to eat during dinners with Iranians. Too little, and they're convinced you didn't like the dish and will race for the kitchen to cook you something else. Too much, and they'll keep loading up your plate until there's no more food. Then the empty plates present a reason to make more food, because clearly you must still be hungry.

It's impossible. A first or second *no* is considered polite banter and will have no impact. When you get to the third or fourth rejection—if handled with the appropriate measure of delicacy—they'll think about believing you. The ability to navigate Persian hospitality requires some fine-tuning if you're used to the self-conscious stylings of British food culture.

It's commonplace to cater for double the number of guests attending for a meal. This happens daily in Iranian households across the world, and it's a habit that reveals the most fundamental components of Persian hospitality: kindness, warmth and, well, gluttony. More than enough food appears on the table, always, just in case an unexpected visitor drops in at dinner time.

Quality and variety are just as important as quantity. A typical Persian dinner spread will feature an oversized plate of rice, a meat dish balanced with just the right mix of herbs and spices, a pile of flat-breads, an overflowing bowl of *maast-o khiar* (Greek-style yoghurt brimming with diced cucumber, fresh mint, salt, and pepper), and a simple salad, often made in the *Shirazi* way (diced cucumber, tomato and onion—hold the lettuce).

In essence, Iranians don't make meals, they make feasts. The dinner table in a Persian home is the place that defines it best.

• • •

My memories of childhood are defined by my heritage. My father was born in Iran and is the youngest of seven children. He and his brothers and sisters are now spread out across the world, but no matter where you are, to be part of this culture is to hold two vital components in particularly high esteem: food and family. I was raised in Britain, but throughout my life my relatives have infused me with the importance of these concepts. My dedication to them lets me know that I am Iranian at my core. No matter which other connections to Iran may have been lost for my father and me, food, like family, is not one of them. We still have the appetites of true Persians.

• • •

My parents have come over for dinner, and my father is lurking in the kitchen, as he always does. Whenever I make Persian food, it's his unspoken duty to shuffle around uncomfortably, peering across the tabletops to supervise my work. Any attempt at conversation is punctuated with his practical, well-meaning interjections.

"Stop, don't put the coriander in yet. Wait until it boils."

"Don't add too much water, let me see."

I protest like a grown-up daughter should, but, truthfully, I love having him here in my kitchen. This typically Persian interference over food is one of the few ways he openly honours his Iranian heritage. And mine.

Out of the corner of my eye, I see him pick up a pomegranate from the fruit bowl. He holds it in his palm for a second, delicately, then gives it a hard squeeze. He runs his fingers over its tough, pink-red skin and frowns slightly. The look on his face tells me he's thinking of Iran, remembering something.

"Are you okay, *baba*?" I ask.

He nods, slowly, without looking up, and pauses a second before speaking. "Do you know that pomegranates are everywhere in Iran? They grow on trees all over the place."

"I didn't know that. Do you like them?"

I busy myself with stirring pots and adjusting temperatures as I speak, conscious of how easily these moments can be lost. If I seem overly interested, if I ask the wrong question, he'll quickly back out of the conversation—a sarcastic comment or a bad-taste joke to conclude the exchange.

"Yes," he replies, transfixed by the pomegranate in his hand. "We call them *anar* in Farsi."

I nod with measured interest.

"In the summer, we used to buy them from the street stalls in Tehran, your aunts and uncles and me. We'd push the skin until all the seeds popped, then suck all the juice out from one little hole in the top. Real pomegranate juice, nothing like the pre-packaged stuff at Sainsbury's."

"Really? How do you do it?" I ask.

"Come over here."

He puts a pomegranate in my hand and we stand there together, squeezing at the sides of the fruit until we feel the seeds go slack under our fingers. I pull a sharp knife from the block and pass it to him. Just one small incision lets everything begin to drip out. By the time we've finished sucking on the juice, our chins are sticky and rouged with pomegranate. Seed escapees are stuck to the bottoms of our feet and scattered across the laminate of the kitchen floor.

My dad looks like a naughty child, standing there with his stained face and gleeful grin. He looks happy.

• • •

We're still sticky with pomegranate when we sit down for dinner. At the table, feasting on the food of my father's homeland, I feel more connected to him, and to my heritage. It's how I always feel after one of these moments with him.

Food and family. That's what Iran is to me.

And that's okay for now.

BIRD IN THE HAND

by Rosa Valerie Campbell

AT the station, everyone waits holding bits of Christmas. It is thirty-nine degrees Celsius and sprouts, baubles and puddings sweat in the heat. Outside the ticket office, the plastic Jesus in the nativity melts into his manger. And I am about to take a frozen turkey on a two-hour train journey with my sister.

Claire arrives, laughs at me carrying the bird like an infant.

"Oh my God, congratulations on your brand new baby!" Then she wipes her brow. "Hot enough for ya?"

"The bird will cool you down," I say. She places it on her hip and coos at it.

"Bird is the word." We both smile. Teeth.

The turkey is so big it occupies its own seat, sits deadly between us. I think: *Sister, you're beautiful.* She thinks the same but our sister-powers were shaken out of us early on and so we can't read each other's minds any more. I can't even reach across to squeeze her hand because of the poultry barrier.

The train rushes into the valley where we grew up and the turkey lurches forward. Out the window, all around is green, green, silver-green of majestic eucalypt forest.

"Do you think there'll be fires this year?"

"Hope not." We both remember the last bad bush fires, back in '97 when the valley blazed in a way that was almost Biblical. We drove home through the twisted and the black to our house, somehow spared.

"Mum's not worried," says Claire.

"Mum's never worried."

We lurch into the station and the turkey falls onto the floor, helpless on its back. The green carpeted seat is wet with turkey juice.

"The infant has wet itself," says Claire.

We arrive at Mum's and she's hosing down the back fence, the barrier between her and the wilderness.

"Hi girls, I gotta finish this now, moderate fire warnings just came through."

Inside, I check the sink for glasses as usual. There are three. I smell them: Water. Lime cordial. Whiskey. I dig my nails into Claire's arm, whisper into the pink shell of her ear. "Fucking hell Claire, Mum's fallen off the wagon."

I let her go; she stumbles forward and whacks her hip on the bench.

"Ouch! Fuck, Jo!"

I hug her quickly and kiss her cheek. "Sorry, I just…"

Mum is wearing slippers on the roof and I wonder if she's drunk. I place the offending glass on the bench. It catches the light and shoots rainbows across the room.

"Pretty," Claire says. I'm jealous for the millionth time of her optimism.

Every night we would watch the show. Witness Mum's drunken euphoria cascading into anger, the full force of it eventually directed at us. Then, when it was finally over, Claire would climb into bed with me and often reveal a creature: "I just found this kitten in the park, let's keep it. Look at its soft fur!"

You have no idea how many times I have heard my sister say, "Look at my new mouse."

A tiny bit of whiskey glows brown in the bottom of the glass. I think of Claire's menagerie.

• • •

"Where's your Xmas jumper?" your mum asks me.

We arrive at your parents' house to fifteen people drinking hot chocolates from matching cups and wearing tasteful Christmas jumpers.

While you kiss your Aunty Irene, I put our bags down in your brother's old room and lie on the bed next to the Eminem poster for four precious minutes before the forty-eight hours of back-to-back Christmas activities begin. *Where's the booze?* I think, which startles me. *But come on, it's Christmas—where the fucking fuck is it?* I feel some solidarity from Eminem at least, with his Valium dependency.

The first activity is making dough into stars, penguins, and cats and then piping on miniature details in icing. I subtly decorate my cat with a Palestinian flag in icing, which makes you smile. "At least your cat has a Xmas jumper on!" says your mum.

• • •

The door clatters behind us and Claire and I both start.

"This house makes me fucking jumpy."

Claire nods and I can see the big heart of my baby sister in her mouth. Mum gets out a bottle of Shloer from the fridge. Shloer, grape juice in champagne-shaped bottles, fizzy water dressed up as almost-wine, she guzzles them all the live-long day.

Last time I visited I opened the cupboard and found six bottles of "wine" with pictures of smiling Muslim couples on them, toasting Mum. *Eid Mubarak!*

"They're from Ahmed from my AA group," she said.

"Great?"

Claire takes my hand. We both look down and I think how many times? How many times have we confronted our mother while staring at our feet, how many different shades of nail polish have I worn? Right now Claire is wearing pastel blue, which looks good, if a bit hypothermic.

I start because I always start: "We found the glass."

"What?"

"The glass in the sink."

"Oh that! Oh girls. It was for the Christmas pudding! You have to stop being so paranoid."

Claire goes to Mum, takes her hand.

"I'm not going to drink again."

Mum strokes Claire's hair. They walk out the back together and I'm left with nothing but the turkey for company.

"What do you think?" I ask the turkey. It doesn't have an opinion.

I squeeze the turkey into the fridge. As I close the door, the Serenity Prayer wobbles in place underneath the fridge magnets. God, it begins, in gold-tipped letters. A pastel sunset is reflected in a lake. I stare at it and wonder: *Our fridge used to be covered in Rothkos— Mum's favourite. Did she trade in taste for sobriety?*

I hold the glass up to the light, examining it for my mother's lip prints. I can't see any and my heart unclenches its hard-knuckled fist. I lick the whiskey out of the glass, my pink tongue snaking downward, wet and animal. Then I think: *she could have rubbed off the lip prints.* And the clench of doubt is back.

• • •

On Christmas Eve I peel potatoes with your mum. Her hand is deep inside the turkey. She stuffs it with mince, rosemary, lard, garlic.

"Do you have all the traditional Xmas food in Australia," she begins to ask. "Like turkey and what not?"

"Yes." My hands are wrinkled from the starchy, freezing potato water.

"Strange, that! Must be hot to make a roast. You could just put all the ingredients out in the sun and wait for them to cook, really, couldn't you?"

Maggie, I think, *you don't know the half of it.*

• • •

On Christmas Eve the firetail finches travel together in fours and call out *Fire!* in their way: *weep-weep ip weep-weep ip*. They smell it long before the news starts broadcasting severe warnings.

"God grant me the serenity," Mum says.

Claire and I hose the roof and fill the guttering with water. We sit out the back, fan ourselves with rolled-up copies of the TV guide and knock back the last of Ahmed's "wine." I wonder if the bush is about to burst into flames around us.

The last time we had to evacuate, Claire nearly died because she went back for a baby roo. I drove us to Sydney because Mum was too trashed and screamed at Claire for most of the way. Claire took off her nighty to wrap up the freezing joey, imitating a kangaroo pouch.

We wait but the evacuation notice doesn't come.

• • •

We all sit down to Christmas dinner together. Outside it begins to snow, like a postcard Christmas. Like a snow globe. Your mum takes the turkey out of the oven. *Ta-da!*

Your dad carves the enormous bird, an excuse for him to use a small electric chainsaw.

You squeeze my thigh under the table and whisper, "I love you," as you pour gravy on my potatoes.

Later, your dad makes everyone troop outside to look at the Christmas lights he has strung up. He flicks the switch but nothing happens. We all watch our breath condense white in the early darkness. Inside, your dad's getting angry, struggling with the manual and the plug. Outside, everyone shares their anecdotes about the difficulties of Christmas lights.

Your mum hums *ding dong merrily on high* brittlely until she can take it no longer: "Want some help?"

"No!" he yells at her.

Finally the lights do their little epileptic dance and everyone claps. He comes outside and they blink off again.

"It's because they're fucking solar." He looks accusingly at your mum. "You're the one who suggested it Maggie, *better for the environment*, but not if they don't fucking work. Fucking green swindle!"

"Don't worry, Gray. I'll just pop to ASDA in the morning."

He cuts his eyes at her and growls. "Don't be stupid. Christmas is over in the morning, Maggie, isn't it?"

We all go back inside, except for your dad. Still raging about the green swindle, he rips the lights down, bulbs smashing on the ground, the strings of broken lights wrapping themselves around his leg so he has to furiously kick his foot to get free.

• • •

On Christmas morning I wake up to the smell of smoke. It's here. The world is on fire. I run into Claire's room but she's already up, her bed still warm from her body. I can see out the window that the backyard is full of smoke. I go into the bathroom and stand under the shower to soak my nighty. I wrench open the linen cupboard and three bottles of wine and a bottle of whiskey tumble out.

I stand against the door of the cupboard and allow myself ten seconds to dig my fingernails into my palms to recuperate. Then I grab my old Scooby Doo sheets and Claire's butterfly ones and soak them through.

I drip through the house. *"Claaaire? Muuum?"*

I open the back door, sling Scooby Doo round my shoulders, cape style. I rub my eyes and can't believe what's happening is not a bushfire.

• • •

After pudding, it's time for whiskey and your ten-year-old cousin's choice of DVD: *National Lampoon's Christmas Vacation*. I pretend I've never seen it before. Predictably, when Chevy Chase starts the hijinks with the Christmas lights your dad's face goes dark with fury.

"I think we should turn it off now," you say.

The ten-year-old is oblivious. "But this is the best bit!"

Then Chevy Chase falls off the roof covered in strings of hundreds of Christmas lights.

You yell at the boy: "Turn that fucking film off."

For the first time our families resemble each other. I drink my whiskey and then I drink yours.

"Steady on babe," you whisper.

"Fuck you," I whisper back, because you scared him, because my heart is caving in with how much I miss Claire and Mum.

• • •

Mum has made an open fire and thrown the turkey on top of it.

"Apparently it wouldn't fit in the oven," Claire explains. I drape the wet butterflies over her shoulders.

The turkey is raw-flesh pink and charcoal black. I can hear its bones breaking in the heat. The flesh has melted off the carcass in some places.

Mum grins, manic-drunk, and the flames flicker in her eyes. Gone to the land of the damned.

I go inside, get the bottle of whiskey that fell out of the cupboard. I rip the Serenity Prayer off the fridge.

"Where's that from?"

"Mum's secret booze stash."

I crack the whiskey open, take a massive 8:00 a.m. Christmas morning slug and pass it round. Scrunch the Serenity Prayer and chuck it on the fire.

Claire takes my hand and we stand there like princesses in our sheet capes.

"Jo, look." Claire uncurls her hand and shows me a pink-bellied, blue-tongued baby lizard—a tiny miracle of Christmas, sitting in the palm of my sister's hand.

RED BEETS MINGLE WITH POTATO SKINS

by Cindy Matthews

NOMFICTION

THE Buick's bright headlights split the descending dusk. Muriel turns off the ignition before leaning into the backseat to grab a jacket. She hops from the car before crushing a cigarette on the gravel driveway with the sole of her shoe. Her black dress plunges low at the neck and sits snug on the hips. From the open screen door I watch Muriel dip her head into the Buick's trunk. She rolls a walker toward her husband, Edward. She moves stiffly, as though more than just her body gives her pain. It doesn't occur to me to leave my post at the door and assist. If I weren't so pissed off at my parents, I might have noticed the sun slipping like a vat of molten glass down the horizon.

"I'll be there, you old coot," Muriel says to Edward, who stays put on the passenger seat. He plants a hand on the dashboard.

"Well," he huffs, "h-h-h-urry on u-u-up."

Once they're inside, Father throws his arms up and welcomes Edward, then Muriel, with a big hug. Muriel sniffs the air and says, "Beef. My favourite."

One thing I never liked was Father's predilection for bringing home people he'd made friends with while working at the jail near Guelph. Edward has been a guard there since the sale of his butcher shop three years ago. Father is a junior chef in the kitchen. Both despise their jobs yet speak of nothing else. Muriel runs a health food store near the jail.

Father had invited them over without first checking with Mother. "It's important to celebrate Edward's recovery from hip surgery," Father had said. "Don't worry. I'll cook. Just make sure the house is ship-shape." Mother was the sort who began to fuss the week leading up to guests' arrival. This particular Saturday I was trapped at home, grounded for uttering *screw you* when I caught Father cheating at cards the previous night.

To placate Father, I'd offered to help with the evening's preparation. He and I had set up two collapsible card tables in the living room before encircling the arrangement with four mismatched wooden chairs. Our galley kitchen was too narrow to seat guests and the house didn't have a dining room. A red linen cloth concealed the shoddiness of the card tables. A vase of dried hydrangeas sat in the middle of the table. There was no chair set for me. I'd sit on a rocker near the hallway leading to the bedrooms.

Mother had run a vacuum over the floors and shone the taps while Father prepared the meal. An entire day devoted to washing, peeling, chopping, stuffing, slicing, sautéing, and roasting. Strips of pummeled red meat fisted bundles of pickles, onions, bacon, and salt. A cup of butter folded into flour formed a roux for the gravy. Cold, fresh whipped cream infused the layers of a Black Forest torte, its glossy surface sprinkled with curls of chocolate. Nothing but the best for Edward.

After washing her hands, Muriel sits on the chair across from Edward. "The rouladen, they're not as good as I expected," Father says. His cheeks flush radish red.

Father spoons meat and gravy onto the plates. When Edward has to saw into the meat, Father frowns. "See. You should be able to cut rouladen with the edge of a fork. Wait until I get my hands on that damn butcher."

Twenty-four twice-baked potatoes line a pan Father's scrounged from the jail. Specks of diced ham, melted cheddar cheese, and fresh chives dot the potatoes' piped stuffing. Nutmeg fills the air. There's enough food to feed eight Edwards.

At these events, guests aren't offered wine. Father doesn't drink it and expects others don't either. The alcohol choices are lager or Canadian Club on ice. Muriel requests herbal tea because she's driving.

Edward's large nose protrudes from his pocked face. Red and blue spider lines creep along his cheeks. He wears horn-rimmed glasses with thick lenses that make his close-set eyes appear cloudy. A vinegary smell flows from his skin. When he lifts his tumbler to take a sip, ice clinks against his teeth. The sound sets my own teeth on edge.

Muriel seldom scores an opportunity to speak but when she does, her British accent is gentle and soothing. The conversation between Father and Edward falters so she outlines the success of lady's slippers she planted in a new garden. Edward waves his hands and sputters, "Wh-wh-who really c-c-c-cares, Muriel?" Then he starts into another of his stories, the words tripping and colliding, soon turning a two-minute story into ten.

Mother closes her eyes and chews deliberately on the rouladen. Her upper dentures slip as the meat swishes in her mouth. I want to leap from my chair and choke her, the grinding noise is so irritating. Instead I detect the voice of my middle school counsellor whispering advice. Breathe. Don't get so riled. Take deep, deep breaths.

Muriel sighs audibly when Edward butts in again with another tale, something about a prisoner, a bottle, and someone's anus.

"Edward, we're eating now," she says. She tilts her head to her shoulder. "That story can surely wait." Her voice is now barely above a whisper, the sound of a teacher consoling an irate five-year-old.

Edward leans back in his chair and sneers. He mouths the word *fuck*. I wonder how they've been able to remain married so long. He with his goddamned stuttering and she with the righteous head tilt and pursed lips. I imagine her at home, stomping from room to room, trying to avoid the stammering. Shredded beet salad sits in the corners of Edward's lips, dots his pristine white shirt. When Mother sends a bowl around for seconds, no one thinks to ask if I've had enough.

By this time, Edward has sloshed back three whiskeys. He tilts his chair the way the boys in my class do—a giant praying mantis tipping onto its back legs. It seems his hip has turned supple with the steady infusion of booze. His lids turn heavy and his head tilts to one side.

Mother tops up Muriel's cup. She plops in so many cubes the drink becomes three parts sugar, one part tea. Muriel taps the cup with her spoon over and over, oblivious to how maddening the sound is. With the brim to her lips, I can hear her blowing the liquid. The muscles in my back tighten. I check the clock on the wall. My breath chuffs over my teeth as I wonder how much longer until they finally leave.

Father slides two more potato skins onto Edward's plate before pushing from the table. "Time for dessert." Father rubs his palms together. "The highlight of the evening, I'm certain you'll agree." He starts to clear the dishes. His heels pound the floor, his hands somehow managing to juggle the greasy pile without anything slithering to the floor. From the ensuing clatter in the kitchen, it's apparent he's decided to abandon us and has commenced clean up before doling out the cake. Mother invites Muriel downstairs to view the renovations to the recreation room and to check out my display of African animal sketches.

Edward remains at the table. He sniffs his nose a few times before inclining a thumb into a nostril. His lids droop before he begins humming.

"Jesus Christ," I mutter.

"You s-s-s-seem awfully n-n-n-nervous," Edward says, his eyes still shut.

I don't answer. I chase bits of food around my plate with the tines of my fork. The red beet salad has bled across the surface and mingled with the potato skins, leaving a river of rouge. My pockets are stuffed with rejected chunks of rouladen. I consider heading to the bathroom to flush the mauled meat. Then maybe I'll offer to do dishes—an olive branch of sorts.

An unexpected pocket of body heat warms the air next to my arm. It's Edward. He's managed to abandon his nose-picking long enough to push off his chair and come within inches of mine. He boosts himself from the walker and inches even closer, so that he has squeezed between me and the bathroom. I stand up, the plate clutched in my hand, not knowing where to go, how to get there, what to say.

"I know-I know-just wh-wh-what you need." Edward yawns and when his jaw clicks, it sounds like a toilet flushing. "Ci-Ci-Ci-Cindy, you're l-l-looking g-g-g-good, you know."

The last time I was home when Edward and Muriel visited was last summer. I'm a lot taller now and my flat chest has sprouted breasts the size of walnuts. I'm wearing a grey T-shirt with a picture of *Pink Floyd* on it. It has faded and shrunk over time. A strip of bare skin pokes from above my jeans. I tug at the base of my shirt, willing it to stay down.

Before I realize what's happening, Edward clamps a hand on my arm. His glasses fog up and I can smell whiskey and onions mixing on his breath. I tip my face away. When I try to wiggle from his grip, his fat fingers tighten around my thin forearm. The seat of the rocker catches the back of my knees, causing my balance to falter. His lips moisten as his tongue darts in and out. The sweat pools in my armpits. And I begin to wonder where Mother and Muriel could still be.

Edward's breath quickens before his chest thumps against

me. His hand now clutches the back of my head while his other encircles my chin. A ring snags my hair. His sloppy lips fold over mine. They fasten on and don't let go. For a broken man, he's strong and determined. His tongue is the texture of beef liver. He layers it between my teeth so I can no longer breathe.

I have to get away, so I nudge my shoulder against his barrel chest but he cements his grip. His lips continue to hoover mine. The enormous mouth manages to vacuum my nostrils, too. I can't speak or breathe. So I tip the plate still clutched in my right hand and smear it against his white cotton shirt.

"F-f-f-fucking bitch," he says, pushing my chest so hard I collapse into the rocker. He shuffles back to the table, wagging his head with each footstep.

I look up. There's Father. His eyes mingle with mine. The glass platter sporting the Black Forest torte slips from his fingers. The cake slumps off the platter onto the red linen tablecloth. Flecks of chocolate and cherry splatter Edward's shirt. "I'll get something to clean you up, Edward." Then Father calmly pivots and goes back into the kitchen. Nervous laughter floats out to us, a sound akin to wind chimes jingling in the breeze.

It's unclear if Father has absorbed what just occurred. If I were ever to bring it up again, he'd say Edward's just not that sort. The sort who delights in forcing a tongue into the mouth of a twelve-year-old. The sort who fantasizes about a pubescent's legs locked around his waist. The kiss shall remain hushed, something closeted between Edward and me. An ache grips my stomach while my socked feet remain stuck to the floor like a piece of dried gum.

THE DINNER PARTY

by David Burga

TILAPIA FILETS — 4

"What's for dinner, Papi?"

"Ceviche," I say.

My son's voice is punctuated by his stamping feet. "I. Want. Grilled. Cheese!"

I ignore him and carefully cut the fish into little cubes. Grilled cheese is my go-to meal for the kids. I feel guilty every time I peel the wrapper from the orange squares that are closer to plastic than they are to food.

I can see Ava standing on the ottoman in the reflection of the kitchen window—at seven years old, it's something she knows she isn't allowed to do. She screams to her little brother as she dives onto the couch. "Hurry! There are giant fish in the ocean!"

Alex joins her and they pretend to catch our dinner. They proudly bring their imaginary fish, held between thumb and forefinger, over to the counter.

I throw the fish—real and imaginary—into a Pyrex dish.

LIMES — 6

The doorbell rings—my parents have arrived. I wouldn't normally invite them over on a school night, but as soon as I'd abandoned the grilled cheese idea, I decided to make it a family event.

"Abuelita!" Ava jumps off the couch. The imaginary ocean disappears.

"Abuelito!" Alex runs down the hallway, after his sister. He slips on the tiles but catches his balance before he falls. He's only recently outgrown socks with rubber on their soles.

My father sits on the couch and Ava jumps into his lap. My wife brings him a beer and even though it's a twist-off he asks Ava to bring him a bottle opener. He holds my daughter's wrist and demonstrates how a lever works, the engineer in him never resting. My mother joins me in the kitchen. She washes her hands and starts pulling out the bigger pieces of fish, slices them in half.

"If you slice the fish thin, like sashimi, it cooks faster."

"Okay," I say, even though the fish doesn't technically "cook."

I haven't intended for my mother to help, but I am slow

getting dinner ready and I could use her expertise. I cut the first lime. My mother picks up a piece and squeezes it over the fish. She flexes her fingers, trying to stretch the pain out of her arthritic hands. She tries again but the lime retains its semispherical shape. I take it from her.

"It's okay, Mami. I'll get it." I put it between my palms and press hard, trying to distribute the juice.

"Don't forget to scoop out the pulp."

My wife calls out from the living room. "Yeah, don't forget to scoop out the pulp-o!"

My wife's running joke is that any English word can be made Spanish by adding an -o to the end of it. My mother laughs because *pulpo*, in Spanish, means octopus.

CELERY HEARTS — 4 TABLESPOONS

"What the hell are celery hearts?"

My mother shakes her head and shows me the bottom of a stalk. The part we always throw away. She cuts thin lines into it, parallel to the length of the stalk, until it resembles a paintbrush. Then she cuts perpendicular to the bristles and makes a small pile of millimeter-sized cubes. She scoops them up and sprinkles them on the fish.

"This is the secret ingredient."

"Really?" The bottom of the celery stalks don't seem capable of locking in much flavour. They can't even lock in any colour. Yet, for a recipe so simple, so many places I know have screwed up ceviche. It feels so cliché to say that the best ceviche in town comes from my mom's house, but whenever my friends ask where they can get some, that's what I tell them.

SALT — ~~2 TABLESPOONS~~ TO TASTE

"Stick out your hand."

I place my palm in front of her and she pours salt out from a box.

"Now sprinkle it around."

But I don't. Instead I pour it into a measuring spoon and then distribute it. I refill the tablespoon and it is only three-quarters full.

"No!" My mother pulls my hand away from the dish before I can empty it out. "I said *to taste*. Did you taste it?"

I laugh. "You're standing right here. Did you see me taste it?"

"No!" She dips a finger into the juice. "It's fine." She dumps the rest of the salt into the sink.

RED ONION — 1 QUARTER, THINLY SLICED

I am staring up at the top of the window frame. My mother cuffs me on the back of the head. "Stop that!"

"Stop what?"

"I know what you're doing. You used to do that as a boy when you did your math problems."

She's right. I was reducing the ratios in my head to single servings—6 limes to 4 tablespoons of celery hearts to 1 tablespoon of salt for 4 tilapia fillets is $1\frac{1}{2}$ limes, 1 tablespoon of celery hearts, and $\frac{1}{4}$ tablespoon of salt per fillet.

"I said taste it."

"Mami, when you were my age, you had two kids in high school, two kids in university and you'd been making ceviche for more than half your life. This is my first time. It'd be way easier if I had a recipe."

My mother channels her inner Jedi Master. "Trust your instincts."

"Okay." I dip a finger into the salty lime juice, a marinade sold in Peru as *leche de tigre*, or tiger's milk, a delicacy and a cure for hangovers.

"If it tastes bitter then you squeezed the limes too hard."

The juice has the right mix of citrus and salt.

"Now, take the onion and slice it as thinly as possible." My mother stands over the onion and the knife slides through the quartered piece. She does a few more and then hands me the knife. I close an eye, staring down the blade, gauging the thickness of the slice and the distance from my fingertips. My mother doesn't have the issue of depth perception since the glaucoma blinded her right eye.

I go slower than my mother and the slices are thicker, but they do the job. My mother separates the layers into individual crescents, scoops them up, and puts them in a strainer. She flicks up the faucet and cranks it all the way to the left. She sticks her hand into the running water.

"You want the water to be super hot. Feel."

I stick my fingers into the stream and then yank them out of the scalding water. My mother's hand is still there, a reminder that mine are only office-tough. She runs the onions under the hot water for a few seconds then douses them in cold water.

"This gets rid of the strong oniony taste."

CILANTRO — 1 TABLESPOON

My mother points the tiny bushel at me and sucks her teeth. "Still?"

"Still what?"

"This is parsley." She shakes her head. "See how the leaves are different and it doesn't smell like cilantro? Just rub the leaves." I delayed many ceviche dinners as a teen after mistakenly bringing home parsley instead of cilantro.

My mother walks down the hallway. She returns with a plastic grocery bag and pulls out a fresh bunch of cilantro. "I came prepared."

I laugh and take it from her. I grab a handful of leaves and chop them as finely as I can, then sprinkle them over the fish and onions.

CHILL AND SERVE

I pop the ceviche into the freezer while we wait for the rice and corn to finish. My mother helps me set the table and I open a bottle of Chilean Chardonnay. We dish up the food and everyone sits.

"Salud," I say.

Everyone digs in.

"Very good, hijo," says my father, who has never been one to sugarcoat his opinion. I agree, though. It tastes just like Mom's, even though I know that, left alone, I'll botch this dish several times before perfecting it.

"I only quarter love it, Papi." Ava is learning fractions in school. Watching her hide all the little pieces of fish in her rice, I am reminded of myself as a child.

My mother winks at my daughter, something she never did with me as a boy. Times were different then. Sacrifices were made. When she would yell at my sisters and me for not eating our food, we had no idea how tough things were, that food not eaten was scarce money wasted.

Our early days in Canada were a kind of exile for my parents. In the pre-Internet years, Christmases, births, birthdays, deaths, and funerals were events that could only be experienced by phone or via the weeks-long time delay of mail. Spontaneous Wednesday night dinners with my grandparents never happened as they were a continent away. But there came a point when my parents' time spent in Canada was greater than their time spent in Peru, and a time when the longing to go back was eclipsed by the potential of a new home.

Sitting with my parents now, I know this is what they wanted for us. I look at my children and they smile. We talk and laugh and drink. Tonight, we celebrate as a family.

TWO TABLES

by Madeleine Leznoff

IF you ask Grandma, they're blintzes, or *blini* as they call them in the old country. She folds the ricotta into the cream cheese with a spatula to make a sweet, cumulus filling. You go to the basement, where the jars of blueberry jam on the shelves are deep bruises between vessels of rubied pickled peppers and silvery herring, all labelled with strips of surgical tape. You choose an opaque jar, almost black, because the jam is thick and will rest gracefully on the steaming pockets.

If you ask Omi, a hemisphere away, they're *pfannkuchen*, meant to be sprinkled with sparkly brown sugar, cinnamon and applesauce, then rolled loosely, and decorated with dollops of whipped cream. Both grandmothers ladle pale batter onto inverted cast iron pans on the stovetop, and in both kitchens, the liquid runs to the end of the edgeless dome and hangs on the horizon. Then it solidifies into a golden sheet and peels off like a perfect sticker.

• • •

At public school, you're the expert on latkes and the Maccabees. With a snap of your forefinger and thumb, you send a dreidel whirling off the wooden desk. You hand out gold chocolate coins and everyone wants to learn how to play.

Other times you carry plates of German cookies to class and point out the different kinds: *Zimtsterne*, the cinnamon and almond stars Mom let you paint carefully with egg whites; the crescent mooned *Vanille Kipferl* covered with icing sugar; *Ausstecher*, the lemony shortbread pressed into angels and snowflakes. Some kids laugh at the names; teachers say they're pretty enough to be sold in bakeries.

• • •

In a small town outside of Stuttgart, nestled at the foot of rolling green hills growing heavy grapes that your mom mischievously plucked as a girl, you sit three floors up in Omi and Opa's dining room for lunch. The table is covered with a starchy, white tablecloth free from wrinkles; it falls symmetrically off the corners in crisp folds. A pyramid of bratwurst, three different salads, and a pot of *spätzle* with lentil stew wait patiently. Before lunch, you watched Omi grate the floury dough into a pot of boiling water and waited for the little dumplings to surrender to the surface.

There is too much food, as always. The potato salad squeaks when tossed in its oil and vinegar dressing, as it should, and the bratwurst snaps between your teeth. You try not to leave scraps. As a kid you saw Opa finish an entire apple, including the core, and a lemon slice with the peel. During the war they had nothing, Mom told you later. In the four years since you last saw them, Omi and Opa have become variations of your memory, like they've slipped quietly out of the solid outlines that existed in your mind when you thought of them. They're thinner: Opa moved his wedding band to his middle finger, but it still slides down to his knuckle when he pours the wine. Everyone is supposed to speak louder, although with your rusty German you barely speak at all, except in smiles and enthusiastic nods, with laughter. You can still understand. You take more salad and more spätzle, until it's impossible to stomach more. Then you wait ten minutes and accept another spoonful.

After lunch, while the coffee brews, you all gather in the living room and lean over a crisp album of black and white photographs of relatives. Opa points out people in family portraits, and you notice how they sit with such straight spines. Their faces glow like moons. Stopping at one page, he tells you, "I think their kids live in Berlin now." He flips the page and says, matter-of-factly, "He died in the war," and points at a photograph on the opposite page: "They moved to America, maybe you could find their grandchildren on the Internet?"

A warm breeze flows through the windows and it's not the flowers blooming wildly all around the apartment building that you smell, but rather the sharp scent of the soil they're planted in. You hear the laundry flapping in the wind and picture it half-pirouetting in the sunlight, held at the shoulders by wooden clips. You wonder if the flowers bloomed during the war, if anyone tended to them. Did the laundry dance then, too? You wonder what it smells like here in the winter.

• • •

Back home, most Sunday nights are spent at your grandparents' house. In their dining room, the table is draped with a creamy tablecloth that gets tossed in the washing machine after dinner, and spills are abundant: the red wine, the gravy, a smear of margarine meant for the *challah*. The cloth becomes a map, a topography that could be studied to piece the whole evening back together. The semi-circle of crumbs collected where your brother sat; the drops of merlot rained from Grandpa's glass when he laughed.

The cabinets in the corners host relics from the decades. Your eyes always settle on something new: blue china platters that have never felt food, blown glass vases from a trip to Venice, or a set of gold-rimmed teacups lined up like soldiers, all their elbows angled identically. You stare into the dark, oily paintings of forests and rivers hanging around the room.

The silver folding chairs are carried up from the basement to squeeze in all the great-aunts and uncles on special occasions. On those nights, Grandma rushes to and from the kitchen with plates of *kugel* and slivers of turkey glistening on lettuce beds. You have to tuck in your elbows to cut your food, and you spend more time passing around dishes than eating. You serve each other with shiny ladles and enormous three-pronged forks. *How many pieces do you want? One, two? Take three!*

You wonder, of course. At Passover Seder, you take two slices of tangy Gefilte fish loaf and watch your brother struggling with his sliding yarmulke across the table, and the thought flits from ear to ear. You think: *in different times, in other circumstances, would you have been the first to hide?* You tell yourself you were born when you were born, because of history, not in spite of it. Change one thing in the past and the whole present shifts. But still. *What if?*

• • •

Your fourth grade teacher scrawls *Holocaust* on the chalkboard in cursive and you watch the letters loop together so easily. She turns to the class and you see the words, the things that you are, shoot out of her mouth into the air in bold and italics. You want to raise your hand to ask *What if I'm both?* But you don't want to step into the light. A knot begins to grow in your stomach, frayed with sadness, wound with guilt and the inevitable questions. Do you want to trace your roots through the soil?

• • •

In the cabinet above the stove, your mom's cookbook collection ranges from *The Joy of Jewish Cooking* to a German cookbook filled with penciled notes you squint to read. She makes latkes at Christmas and the smoke from the bubbling oil fills the whole house with a greasy haze that stings your eyes. You laugh and open the windows, the front door to let it escape. You eat squeaky potato salad with cucumbers in the summer, and noodle kugel with apple and cranberries in the winter. Your parents broke a glass beneath their feet to shouts of *Mazel Tov!* at their wedding; they bowed their heads to cheers of *Prost!* before tasting the wine. The dance floor felt the tiptoe of the waltz and the bouncing of the Horah.

• • •

You taste the recipes of your ancestors at two tables; in each seat, you feel whole in different ways and more so with every bite. It's later, when you've left the dining room, that you consider the similarities and the differences: the lack of salt, the added salt, the portions, the gentle garnishes. At two tables, over different cloths, you savour the tastes. You take seconds. One day, the cookbooks will find a way into your kitchen, and you'll try to read the cursive in the margins.

HANDMADE

by dee Hobsbawn-Smith

WHEN my sons were small, I often took them to the fabric store. Dailyn, my youngest, would run his fingers over waterfalls of satin, velvet like ripe peaches, the slubby resistance of silk, assessing texture and drape with the touch of a born connoisseur. As a five-year-old, his colour preferences leaned toward bright yellows smeared like broken eggs over charcoal, but even then he knew instinctively that knowledge resides in the hands. Back at home, I pinned, cut, then sat down at my Elna and whirred pieces of cloth into archers' tunics, wizards' robes resplendent with comets and starbursts, jazzy tasselled two-toned jesters' hats. We played made-up games in made-up countries, with made-up characters, attired in our fantastical outfits.

Each boy gravitated toward my chefs' whites as they hung in my closet after laundering, smelling of fresh air instead of garlic or onions. He would wrap the mark of my trade around himself, lost in the folds of material, plucking at the knotted cloth buttons marching down the jacket-front as he paraded down the hallway to the kitchen. It wasn't that my whites or what they represented were mysterious, or foreign territory to them. Far from it. My sons were intimately acquainted with the landscape of food, and my chef's uniform was the most comfortable and comforting clothing they knew.

• • •

Dailyn, visiting from Calgary, finds me in the kitchen of the old Saskatchewan farmhouse I now live in. He takes the bowl of bread dough from my hands, plops it on the counter, yards off his sweater to reveal a baker's biceps. "Here, let me," he says, dusting his hands with flour and starting to knead, hands working in a double-time crossover-rhythm that is smooth and effective, rapid, unhurried.

"It's a braided Finnish bread called *pulla*," I tell him. "Five strands, like challah."

"Show me. I don't know how." So I roll ropes of dough, fold the ends, interweave the strands, chanting the braiding sequence like a mantra: two over three, five over two, one over three. After I finish the first loaf, he steps in. "It looks a bit rough, Mom."

"Been awhile."

"Yeah? It shows." As he rolls and shapes them, the ropes are well behaved, mooring themselves one to the next without twists or tangles, as guylines heed a skilled deckhand. Within minutes, he's made seven loaves, each snug and matter-of-factly tidy, waiting to bloom in the oven under a tempera-like glaze of egg yolk and cream. His hands on the dough are sturdy, not as delicate or as long as his brother's piano-playing fingers, but workmanlike, an artisan's hands, fine-tuned through the generations for doing, making, gauging, assessing. When he catches me studying him, he winks and flexes his left arm. "I make bazillions of buns and loaves every morning at work," he says with unabashed pride. An hour later, when the loaves emerge from the oven, he pulls apart the intricacy of the crusted braid with fingers as facile as a jeweller's, sniffing delicately—a rabbit assessing a carrot crop before tasting. "That's cardamom I can smell under all that butter, right?" Between us, we consume half a loaf while it is still warm.

• • •

If flour is of earth, and water is water, then yeast is of air—that which elevates. Fire is the element of transformation, what magicks the other three. Cooks know this, are drawn to gas ranges, woodstoves, open-flame barbecue pits, beachside grills, anywhere fire is visible. That transformation—the heating blast of the sun and its hint of the Beyond—turns raw ingredients into dinner, untutored children into young men and women, citizens of clay into golden heroes. Fire is the cook's first and best tool. Life is the crucible.

• • •

Both my sons outgrew my whites years ago. They wear their own each day, both in the same restaurant—one the baker, the other a line cook. I visit them at work, sit at the counter on the guests' side, my boys a world away from me in the open kitchen that is the restaurant's nerve centre. Darl, his face covered with shining beads, is at the wood-fired rotisserie, its heat drawing sweat from me ten feet away. He sets down my plate, crosses his arms, leans against his side of the counter, studying my reaction as I slice through the hash marks of tender grilled scallops perched on a quarter-head of grilled romaine dressed in olive oil, capers, and lemon zest. "Good, eh?" I nod, my mouth full. Dailyn delivers molten chocolate tart and ice cream and cookie and coulis, elements arranged on the white plate like art, then hangs around, grinning, as I match up textures, bite by bite.

Cooking is an intensely physical profession, drastically underpaid for the stamina, skills and contribution it demands. I don't expect either of them to make it their life's work, and have encouraged them to have a plan, a skill beyond the stove so they can exit the kitchen before they hit thirty-six, as I did. Their adult years in commercial kitchens have already wrought changes in them, changes that began inside and manifested outwardly, as bulging biceps and muscular hands, as tough skin that seems impervious to hot pans, as the grace of dancers pivoting at the stove, as calmness when pots boil over and flames gutter out. Over and over again, I remind myself that they are independent beings, young men responsible for their own growth and wellbeing. It's difficult to remember, though, whenever they call in an upset, their voices raised or strained, to rant about the long hours and poor pay of their chosen jobs. Electricians, carpenters, and plumbers earn double or triple a well-paid line cook's hourly wage, without the exposure to hot ovens, deep fryers filled with searing oil, seven-hundred-degree rotisseries. I struggle to remember then that my sons have chosen paths that fit their ethos, that paths take turns, labyrinthine at times, without obvious endpoints, the maze's core invisible during day-to-day living.

We—my sons and siblings and I—are descended from off-colony Hutterites, peasant pacifists renowned in central Europe not just as farmers but also as artisans. One of my brothers makes wooden furniture, the other is a metal sculptor; my sister has spent years at a potter's wheel, throwing clay into useful and gorgeous shapes. My hands, formed from the same last, have the same shape and look of my grandmother's, and of my youngest son's. It's a gift you are born with, to have the hands of a maker, to be grounded in the natural world, to take primal elements and shape them, transform them, and in the doing, serve as the focal point and translator for those at a remove from the natural world. It's not independence, although when I see my sons standing tall in front of the stove, I see their self-reliance glowing around them like an aura; it's interdependence. In cooking, we express our deepest feelings about the nature of the universe, our deepest faith and connection to all that is primal and irresistible. In cooking, we express our choices—to link with nature, to be self-reliant, able to care for others, to manifest the humility and generosity we were born into. But cooking for a living isn't the only way to experience any of those realities.

• • •

Darl was seven, Dailyn three, when my husband and I bought a restaurant. Thirty-seven seats, a split-level with a pair of elaborately carved carousel ponies mounted on the spindle railing of the divider. Fading hardwood floors, pressed-back chairs, Key Largo fans and floor-to-ceiling windows—a joint Lauren Bacall would have been comfortable in. A small four-burner Wolf range sat at the heart of the cramped kitchen, a convection oven hemming in its heat on one side, stainless-steel dishwasher humming on the other, with just enough space for one person to stand in front of the Wolf. After school that fall, the boys sat on stools at the narrow counter, watching me work, Darl's long legs swinging, Dailyn's stubby calves folded like a nesting bird's. I gave Darl an apple and a short-bladed serrated knife with a rounded tip. "Peel this," I said, and went back to rolling out my pastry.

"What kind of apple is it?" Darl asked, his fair eyebrows climbing as a long comma of peel dangled floor-ward from his fingers. "Can I eat the peel? Is it a Gala or a Newton or a Granny Smith or a Mac?"

"Of course eat the peel! Then taste, and tell me."

He rescued the ribbon of peel, scrunched his face. "Gala," he answered through the crunching, "it tastes like a Gala." He handed his brother a slice. "Try it, Dailyn."

The next summer, during cherry season, I gave them cherries like tiny fairy globes, some golden, some ruby, others so dark a purple they were almost black. In peach season, they ate peaches, clingstone, freestone, juices like melted amber dribbling down their chins. They watched me whisk vinaigrettes, taste sauces, plate salads, and simmer short ribs, build mousses and meringues, then they rummaged in the shelves of the dry stores in the basement prep kitchen, searching for snacks, eating again and again, then going home to their own suppers with our nanny. I read notes from them when I stumbled home late at night, exhausted, reeking of garlic and caramel and roasted meats and coffee. *Mama, we miss you, come cook at home.* I didn't have the words to explain the compulsion that drove me to feed others instead of them, couldn't even explain it to myself. In photographs from that era, my face is haunted, gaunt, my bones almost showing through, my flesh consumed by the fire that fed on my ambition. The compulsion burnt its way throughout my body, and a couple years later, we sold the restaurant. I staggered through several years in a daze, wondering who I was if I wasn't a chef.

• • •

Darl's face is tense, his eyes shadowed, when he arrives on my snowbound farm six hundred kilometres from his apartment. I'm surprised to see him; he and his brother have moved on to working six days a week at a hot new resto in Calgary, a place so jumping that time off is nonexistent. "I quit my job," he says over coffee and a plateful of muffins. "I found myself crying in the dish pit. Couldn't eat. Worrying about work before I went in. I just can't cook at that stress level." He looks at me, knows I'll understand. "I care too much about food to cook for a living anymore, Mom. I want to make things with my hands, but I don't know what." I understand his conundrum, but don't know either, no matter how badly I'd love to have an answer for my boy.

A week later, the muscles that line his face are beginning to relax. He stays up late, communing with the far-off Northern Lights as they lean closer to the earth to hear the coyotes carolling. Like the cats perched on the heat register and rocker in front of the fire, he sleeps in. When he surfaces, I hand him a mug, remembering the years it took me to find myself, the artist separate from the cook. We make supper together. As he dismembers a chicken for the pot, slices an onion, slivers garlic cloves into shards, I am relieved, watching his sure hands wielding my knives. It isn't cooking that has damaged him, but the trade of cooking. His love of making is intact. The path has turned beneath his feet, and will carry him closer to the heart of the maze, to the man he is meant to become.

NIL BY MOUTH

by Alisa Gordaneer

FRIED rice, pumpkin pie, mincemeat tarts. Oatmeal topped with brown sugar, flax seeds, raisins, dollops of yogurt. Licorice allsorts, chocolate squares, toast with marmalade.

• • •

My dad always loved eating. And who can blame him, or any of us? Food brings pleasure, nourishment, a satisfying break from the day's tasks. Accepted wisdom: if you love food, you love life.

Except. Everything changed the day he collapsed on his way to the kitchen for a cup of tea. A massive stroke put him in hospital, unable to walk, barely able to talk. Despite rehabilitation efforts, despite medications, despite the plastic trays of grey roast beef and red Jell-O, he became weaker, not stronger, over the month that followed. My mom and I would visit, ever more concerned. He'd lost strength, interest in eating. Just that lunchtime, he'd coughed and gurgled through a spoonful of hospital-tray yogurt. Most of it ended up down his face, undignified strawberry in his beard. Something was going wrong.

The doctor told us the news in the tiny room behind the nursing station, the one stocked with extra boxes of Kleenex. "We now know the stroke damaged the part of his brain that controls swallowing," he continued, matter-of-factly. "He's aspirating food, and it's getting into his lungs, causing pneumonia. Your dad's a very ill man."

Breathing food. I grew quiet. The thought of choking makes me nervous. I choked on a hot dog as a preschooler, a piece of meat as a teen. My brain can control swallowing, but ever since I have eaten slowly, chewing every bite—a mindful eater long before it became *en vogue*. I eat carefully, even fearfully at times. Felt it again when my toddlers tackled popcorn, steak, raw carrots. And now, with my dad. And yogurt.

"He can't eat anymore." The doctor shook his head, explaining that while the food was causing Dad's pneumonia, it also meant he wasn't getting enough nutrition to fight the pneumonia. To stay alive. "At some point, probably in the next two days, I'll have to intervene."

"To do what?" my mom asked, breaking her worried silence.

There were two options, the doctor said. A nasal feeding tube, while extremely uncomfortable for the patient, might offer a short-term solution. Or, if he became strong enough to endure surgery, he could have a feeding tube inserted directly through his abdomen.

"Only two options?" we asked.

The doctor paused gravely. There was a third. "You can let nature take its course."

• • •

Sandwich generation. It has two meanings: More literally, it's the ongoing preparation of easily consumed food, generating ongoing energy for those who consume it. Less so, it describes people like me, who seem to be the ones actually making all those sandwiches.

When my family first moved in together, forming a three-generation household of kids, parents, and grandparents, my dad joked that he was in the best retirement home ever. And for three years, I had been head chef for our household, while my dad kept up with his fine art painting, and my mom ran her business. Apart from the occasional moment when it became just one more chore on my sandwich generation to-do list, I mostly enjoyed cooking. It was fun to prepare food I knew my dad would appreciate and enjoy. Fried rice. Pumpkin pie. Mincemeat tarts. None of which he would ever eat again?

I stared at the doctor with disbelief. "Will the feeding tube replace all other food? Because I could make purees, bring them to him. Or what about soup?"

The doctor smiled, not unkindly. "You're being a mother," he said. "You have this idea that feeding the ones you love is the only way to make them well."

Isn't it?

"Will it even help?" I asked.

The doctor shrugged. "It's his best shot."

It was, we all knew, his only shot. The food was killing him. Without food, he'd die.

• • •

NPO. *Nil per os.* The notice went up on the whiteboard by Dad's bed. Nothing by mouth. The hospital had decided, on a Friday afternoon, not to risk feeding him until the nasal tube was installed. First thing Monday morning. As the weekend passed, he grew weaker and weaker, his voice barely a whisper, his hands too frail to sign the consent for the procedure. Now he had pneumonia, *and* he was starving. He had to be lifted by sling into his wheelchair.

"It'll be uncomfortable," I told him. "But it might help." I was pushing him across the hospital parking lot, our daily outing. I liked to stop by the bramble bushes to snack on the ripe early September blackberries, sating my own busy-day hunger. This time, I turned him away so he couldn't see me gorge like a bear preparing for hibernation.

I love food, but find it hard to trust. It's not just the swallowing. It's what happens when you eat something that could do you harm. Food that causes pneumonia. Hidden allergens causing anaphylaxis. When I was a teen, both my brother and I ended up in the emergency room after unknowingly eating nuts.

For years afterward, I could eat next to nothing. Too scared to have another allergy attack, I was surviving on rice cakes, apples, black tea. Surviving.

You have to eat to live, I was told. So I added milk, timidly, then corn, then more and more foods. But still, I'd carry emergency antihistamines, read ingredients obsessively, avoid restaurants, say a silent grace before I consumed anything: *This food is safe for my body. I will not die from this food.* Eventually, I learned to cook, partly in self-defense. If I cooked it, it would be safe. If I cooked it, it would keep me—and those I loved—alive.

• • •

On the Monday morning, I arrived while the insertion was happening. Waiting in my car, I sniffled miserably at the thought of my dad wincing while technicians threaded a thin plastic tube through his right nostril, down his throat, into his stomach. I found out later they had to try three times to get it right, to make sure it hadn't slid into his weakened lungs instead, hadn't made a dangerous *J* that would push fluid back up his throat.

The tube was taped to his nose and cheek, veering past his reddened eyes. As uncomfortable as it looked, I reminded myself it was a temporary measure, to be replaced by a permanent tube. Or not replaced at all.

Sitting on the edge of his bed, I broke off a small square from a chocolate bar, popped it into his mouth. The chocolate melted, smeared his lips and teeth, dissolved. Made him cough. Eating it could kill him. I felt scared. Subversive.

As far as either of us knew, it was the last real food he'd ever eat.

Soon, a nurse arrived to administer his first "meal," a condensed-milk can containing a vilely sticky formula. It looked like pale gravy as she poured it into a vinyl bag that dripped the liquid into a tube, through a machine that regulated the flow, and into the tube in his nose.

"Pretend it's roast beef," I joked as it trickled in. "Now pretend it's ice cream and pie. You can't choke. You don't even have to be awake to eat." It took him nearly two hours to consume 250 millilitres. "You're eating even slower than I do, now."

I couldn't help but read the ingredients on the formula can: maltodextrin, corn oil, soy protein isolate, oat fiber, fructooligosaccharides, medium-chain triglycerides, unpronounceable vitamins and minerals and electrolytes. Baby milk for adults—a magic formula that seemed to work. Over the next weeks, he fought off the pneumonia, grew more alert. But the tube down his nose was becoming irritated, and, when half-asleep, he'd try to pull it out. Sometimes he'd succeed, necessitating another uncomfortable insertion.

As soon as he was strong enough for surgery, doctors installed the gastro-tube. "Extreme belly piercing," I joked, the first time I saw it. The tube was strangely comic, a clear plastic tunnel sprouting from the left side of Dad's abdomen. It ended in a Y-shaped device, the branches capped like beach ball valves.

"You'll be easy to cook for, now," I told him. His day's rations were now up to two cans of formula for breakfast, one for lunch, two more for dinner. It kept him alive. Barely. For someone who once lived to eat, was plain nourishment enough?

A month later, he still couldn't walk, still couldn't turn himself over in bed. But the hospital decided it was time to send him home.

"You can do this feeding yourselves," the nurse said. "Just order one case of twenty-four cans to start with—it's expensive. And you can always order more. If you need it."

"If? He might be able to switch back to food when he's home?" I asked hopefully.

She grew silent. That wasn't what she meant. "He can't walk anymore. He can't eat. You have to think about quality of life."

• • •

The day he was brought home, a team of dietitians arrived to show me, my mom—even my ten-year-old—how to attach the gravity feed bag of formula to a borrowed IV pole and then to Dad's tube. How to adjust the valves to keep from splashing formula—or gastric juices—all over the floor.

"Real food is out of the question," said a dietitian. "See that drool? His swallowing reflex still doesn't work. If he aspirates, you're right back to pneumonia."

But he was home. That night, we wheeled him to the dining table, attached the feed bag more or less successfully. While Dad's formula dripped, my mom, the kids, and I ate spaghetti. Everyone wearing brave faces, saying the experience of him being home was nourishment in itself.

As weeks passed, his lingering cough began to vanish. He didn't drool anymore, which suggested he might be swallowing. One night as he sat watching the rest of us eat dinner, I gave him a dab of hot sauce on a spoon, just so he could taste something. His eyes watered, but with pleasure. Soon, he tasted a dab of gravy. Then ketchup. And didn't choke.

Encouraged, his doctor suggested popsicles. Eager to cook something for him, to make him well, I made V8 popsicles, then gravy ones. They didn't make him cough. The pneumonia stayed away. He tried yogurt. It worked. I bought a blender for Christmas, fed Dad pureed turkey dinner. With a spoon. While his formula dripped in through his belly, he ate a whole bowlful.

By the New Year, the chunks in his food began to get bigger. The formula doses became smaller. His neural pathways were rebuilding like a set of new highway overpasses over an earthquake chasm. Like I did by relearning to trust food, his body relearned to trust its own ability to chew, swallow. Slowly. Purees moved to chunks, chunks to whole mouthfuls. Sandwiches, pies, ice cream. Soon, the blender sat unused, and the feeding tube, once so necessary, became redundant.

"I've never done this before," the doctor said when he removed it. Such things are usually a one-way trip.

I made fried rice for dinner that night, the family favourite. We all gathered at the dining room table, hungry and ready to go on living. My dad still in his wheelchair, but devouring every bite.

AND THE SPOON RAN AWAY WITH THE TRASH

by Tanya R. Ward

I'VE seen the same plate in the dishwasher for a week and a half now, which is about as long as it's been since Jack's last day off. The two occurrences are not coincidental. If, during the unloading procedure, I notice a plate—fork, bowl, pot, what have you—that has somehow escaped the cleaning process, I simply put it back. Most often this works to my advantage, since one of two things will usually happen: 1) The dishwasher will eventually erode the baked-on food. 2) The dishwasher will fail to erode the baked-on food within a reasonable amount of time, so Jack will provide divine intervention.

This Sunday is no exception.

• • •

"How long's this dish been in here?" Jack asks, before we cook our eggs. He furrows his brow and scratches at the damning evidence. He knows exactly what I've been up to.

"That one?" I ask.

"Yes, this one." He looks at me, vaguely annoyed.

"I don't know. They all look the same to me." I feign interest in the residue before I busy myself in the fridge. "Looks like the eggs you had last week. Why didn't you rinse it before you put it in?"

Jack is silent. With my head buried in the refrigerator, I'm not sure if that silence has meaning. It seems unlikely for him to forget he never had eggs—that was me. But when you're as busy as Jack—an architect for whom the priorities of life are redrawn as follows: building, family, God—and you've been together long enough to forget the simple things, like how you started sharing socks in the first place, life tends to blend together into one big soupy mess. Which is, incidentally, easily eroded by the dishwasher. Of course, it's equally possible he knows I'm full of shit. Either way, I'd prefer to just ignore the matter.

I spot what I'm looking for—a yogurt cup—and head for the cutlery drawer. The offensive dish is soaking in the sink and Jack is unloading the top rack. I open the drawer to retrieve the appropriate utensil, and notice an alarming absence of spoons in the cutlery tray.

• • •

Years ago my mother would pack my lunch in one of those insulated zip-top bags all the children used to carry. Mine was a self-inflicted somber shade of navy, which I suppose was a reaction to its predecessor—a shade of neon pink so shocking that a cube-shaped after-image was a routine part of my lunch hour. More often than I deserved, she would entrust me with an item from the cutlery drawer to go along with my dessert, usually a container filled with vanilla or chocolate pudding, homemade. There was just one problem with this arrangement: I never knew what to do with the spoon afterward. Even when licked clean with the particularity of a cat, it still retained the adhesive properties of used milk, and the idea of a gummy utensil rolling around in my filthy desk or sullying the inside of my bag was enough to set off my gag reflex—somehow, it would always end up with a thin coating of lint and hair. So—and I'm ashamed to admit it—I would sometimes throw them out.

I felt bad about this every time I dangled the spoon over the classroom garbage can, holding it by the end with two soft fingers and a will as weak as my grip. The trouble was, my best friend Lynn would gurgle with glee every time I did it. I loved that sound, the sound of acceptance and unity, of camaraderie and lunchroom heroism, a sound that evoked feelings far greater than my feelings about any spoon. And so I let them fall, blissfully unaware that with each drop I traded a series of lasting objects for fleeting and momentary laughter.

• • •

I once made the mistake of looking into the garbage can afterward, the image of the solitary, discarded spoon amongst half-eaten apples and plastic wrap all too real, too present. So I reminded myself these weren't exactly spoons from my mother's set—these were their duller, more utilitarian, more suspicious counterparts, the ones with an *S* engraved on the handle (S for Sabena Airlines, or "souvenir," according to my mother)—and banished my guilty conscience until I had the next urge to dispose. Perhaps I believed I was playing God, doling out punishment and speeding along the selection of the fittest. Aesthetically, that is. Or perhaps I was just fooling myself, somehow believing that one spoon here and there didn't matter, couldn't make a difference.

• • •

It wasn't until I was emptying the dishwasher on a Saturday afternoon, reluctantly, at the height of my disposing spree, that I noticed our stock of stolen spoons had dwindled to an obviously low number. I stood there, utensils in hand, mouth forming a perfect *O*. Much like the cigarette butts I would throw over the garden wall at home, many, many years later, it had become apparent that small things can and do add up. And sometimes start a fire. Which, on the plus side, destroys the evidence.

And so, just like that, I stopped.

• • •

I thought I'd gotten away with this unfortunate series of disposals until last month, some two decades later, when my mother approached me in my own kitchen over a glass and a half of wine.

"I've been meaning to ask you…" she said.

"Yes…?" I looked up from the de-corking process, a risky bit of business for someone as uncoordinated as myself. The wine opener was one of those pricey numbers, a happy-looking chrome and plastic doll on the end of a corkscrew that seems innocent enough until you meet your chin with the business end of that smiling face and need stitches. It hasn't happened to me, but it has happened to Jack. Eleven years later and he still can't grow a beard in that spot.

"Do you know what happened to my spoons?" my mother asked.

And once again I was ten years old, standing over the cutlery drawer, mouth forming a perfect O.

"Why would I know what happened to your spoons?" The lie came out of my mouth easily, although the cork was proving stubborn. I worked away at it, moderately grateful for the distraction.

"Because your dad doesn't know what happened to them."

The cork popped. I poured two glasses and nudged one in her direction.

"You know, Mom, I'm pretty sure you always had that many spoons." I took a sip of wine and frowned. It tasted bitter. I looked into my glass and noticed a substantial amount of cork floating on top.

"I counted them," she said.

Of course she did.

• • •

The thing about my mother—and even more so, her mother, and her mother's mother—is this: she generally has a greater understanding of value than I do. Despite vivid memories of running through Toys "R" Us with a twenty dollar bill clenched in my sweaty fist and crying out to anyone who would listen, "I must find something with good play value!", I have thrown out *actual cutlery*, and sometimes, when I stick my heel through a pair of threadbare socks, I colour the air with a few choice words before I deposit those socks, too, in the trash. (In my defense, I have persisted in wearing them and that only results in sticking to the linoleum and embarrassing myself in polite company. Also, one of the benefits of sharing socks with my spouse is that I can always blame him for the holes.) My mother, or surely my grandmother, would have gotten out a darning needle and yarn—whether immediately or not—and mended those socks, thoroughly, satisfactorily, and without complaining.

• • •

This past Christmas, while setting out spoons for our dessert—Sex-In-A-Pan, my grandmother calls it, although I prefer DineSafe names like Mississippi Mud Pie—I placed a spoon in front of Lynn and reminded her about the good old days. She laughed at the memory but this time without glee: I was too lazy, she told our friends, to rinse the spoons and bring them home. An appropriate observation coming from the same woman who, well into her thirties, threw out an entire container of spaghetti, Tupperware and all, because it had gone moldy in the refrigerator. She lamented then, too, as she did now, about how our mothers would surely have emptied and cleaned the container, but she couldn't be bothered, what with how vile it was; whereupon I mournfully agreed and dished out the Mississippi Mud Pie. Plus there was the time it would take, I said in solidarity; and with the enormous amount of water, soap, and bleach needed to clean the pot, wasn't she actually doing the environment a favour?

Oh Jesus, my mother would say. The world is going to hell in a handbasket.

• • •

In a way, Lynn was right that day, her observation keen and apt as always. I *was* too lazy to rinse the spoons and bring them home. But I was also eager to hear her laughter, to bond, to create memories for us to share. It's ironic that, in so doing, I may have contributed to the eventual disposal of those memories as well. What I wouldn't have given for one of those spoons at Christmas to place in front of her, instead of a member from my own set—shiny, new, and as yet meaningless. And what I wouldn't give for one of those spoons when I'm an old woman, and when Lynn, along with my stock of available memories, might be long gone.

Standing before my mother in the kitchen, I ventured one

index finger into my wine and chased a piece of cork around the surface until, finally, I pinned it to the side and dragged it to the rim. I looked up at her, cork pinched between two soft fingers. I was fairly certain she knew; there was a glint in her eyes too early to be the wine, and the right side of her mouth was lifted upwards. Surely I could come clean, I reasoned; I'd have my own children soon enough. Sufficient time had passed to make my actions uncollectable, like invoices that had gone unsent, or even funny, like those pants my grandfather burned at the dump. And surely I ought to come clean. I didn't want my mother looking for those spoons as my grandmother had for those pants. As she continued to look for those pants.

"Ahh…" I said, and laughed, flicking the crumb into the sink. "It's a funny story…"

• • •

I lick the yogurt from my spoon and wonder about the retribution for my actions and the fate of my own cutlery in the hands of my potential spawn. The spoon I'm holding isn't a nice one, exactly, and it doesn't match the rest, but it's part of the set Jack and I had when we rented our first apartment. We used to push the loveseats together and eat cereal within its high walls, facing one another, the soft cushions our own island, complete and hidden from the world. These days, we still eat cereal together, but we eat it side by side, facing out, on a single designer couch. Unlike the previous sofa, the successor is beautiful, but it is also unyielding, akin to the steel and glass structures he exhausts himself to produce. You can't go back, they say. I can't help but wonder if it's worth it, and for how long it will stand.

When I confessed to my mother in the kitchen that day, she didn't scold me. Instead she told me about an old, marked pot my great-grandmother used to have. When my mother was a child, she'd watch her grandmother stand at the sink, washing that old pot, slowly, carefully. And every time, her grandmother would say, "Your grandfather made that mark," and smile into the soap suds. He was long gone by then; she didn't go shortly after.

That's the other thing about my mother. She always knows what to say.

I look at Jack from across the kitchen. He's working at the baked-on eggs, leaning against the counter the way he does when his back hurts. My face softens and I go to the sink. I can't take away my actions, but I can repent. And above all, I can keep my children away from the cutlery.

"Jack," I say, spoon in hand, "When we have kids…"

I drop my spoon into the water and immerse my hands into the soap. It isn't as warm as it should be and for a moment I think about pulling my hands out. But I don't. I keep them right there alongside his own.

"Don't let my mother pack their lunch."

HOW TO PRESERVE
FOOD FOR THE WINTER

by Robyn Ryle

EGGPLANT

Cut the eggplant into small rounds that will roll off the cutting board and onto the kitchen floor. Do not concern yourself with those that disappear beneath the stove to decay. Reflect on the fragility of the plants and the small grace that they survived the flea beetles this year. Heat the oven to a temperature that matches your sense of the summer it has been. Brush them lightly with olive oil. You are an artist. In the heat, their skins will go from purple to gray. This signals that they are ready for the cold of winter. Do not mourn; they will taste better for the memory of what they once had been. Tuck them into plastic bags and put them next to the frozen tomatoes for the Moroccan stew in February. Feel smug, because you are the ant and not the grasshopper. Remember that in Paris, they are aubergines.

CORN

Always boil enough sweet corn so that everyone can have at least two ears. (Even the people who say they only want one ear will eat at least two.) Pick the corn just moments before you shuck it and put it in the pot. Run barefoot across the grass and clover toward the kitchen! Race the fireflies! Move fast! The sweetness is fleeting. The sugar fades with each moment of separation. Cook at least a dozen ears at a time and eat them only with people who have never run away from who they are. Cover a picnic table with a red checked cloth. Always grow white corn. Never yellow. Bigger is not better. Don't let the ears grow lazy and full in the sharp heat of July. Err on the side of childhood and youth. If there are ears left over in the pot afterward, wait until the last light of the summer day has faded from the sky. Return when the sound of children being called to bed drifts in through the window. With a large knife, cut the kernels off the cob. Take pleasure in the way they cling together in flat chunks of neat rows. Put the kernels in a plastic bag and freeze for soup. Tuck corn-sticky hands under your pillow in bed. Dream of the rustle of dried cornstalks with snow at their feet.

BEETS

Eat the greens first, cooked until they grow silky in a pan with a little olive oil, garlic, and the water that lingers after you wash them under the sink. Leave the beets for later, cut off and adrift. Let them contemplate their fate. Let them stare at you like purple eyeballs from inside the vegetable drawer in the refrigerator. See their hairy little roots as tails. Imagine their screams as you cut them off. The dark, red juice is their revenge. Remember the cheap, everyday plates your mother got at a gas station and the purple stains that never washed off from eating pickled beets all summer. Poke the beets in the pan of boiling water and watch the purple liquid stream out. Know that they are still not done. They resist. Slip the skins off as if you are politely taking their jackets at the beginning of a dinner party, but the beets are not fooled. Slice and cook them in vinegar, water and exactly one whole clove. Wipe the beet juice from the counter, the floor, the sink, your hands. Remember your mother's warning—*beet juice stains!* Store them in the fridge for lunch tomorrow. In the morning, find the drop you missed laughing at you on the surface of the kitchen table. Know that with or without you, beets are ancient and eternal.

TOMATOES

Fill your mother's bright green Tupperware bowl with tomatoes. This is how you measure enough for a canner. When the morning mist still hangs low on the river, bring a pot of water to boil on the oven. Call your mother to ask how long you leave the quart jars in the hot water bath. Never write the answer down. Shake your head *no* when your husband asks if you need help. Push your hand hard against your back where it hurts from bending over the sink to pull the skin off the blanched tomatoes. Contemplate whether it was a tomato and not an apple that tempted Eve. Bring each slippery, skinless globe close to your face and inhale deeply to make sure no bad ones get in. Spend the afternoon inside the smell of cooking tomatoes. Become intimate with their delicate construction, the walls and chambers of red flesh. Cut the peeled tomatoes into quarters, slicing toward your hand with the knife, because this is how your mother taught you. Measure a teaspoon of salt into each jar and wipe the rims carefully with a wet paper towel so they will seal. Imagine your mother, standing behind you. Remove each jar from the boiling water bath and wait for the soft popping sound the lids make when they seal. Listen closely. Count each one. Call your mother to report the results when you are done every single time. Know that she is never prouder of you than when all your jars seal. Write the year on the lid with a permanent marker. Believe for a moment that time can be stopped and your mother will always be there to answer when you call.

THE LAST SUPPER

by Rebeca Dunn-Krahn

DESPITE having saved our pennies for years to afford a twelve-month trip to Europe for our family of four, money was tight the entire time, and got tighter in the final months. We put ourselves on a strict daily budget, which I referred to as our "austerity measures." On the last night of the trip, a fancy dinner in downtown Reykjavik was out of the question, so we headed to a grocery store to buy pasta and tomato sauce to cook in the kitchen of our Airbnb basement suite on the edge of town.

As we unloaded the groceries from the back of our rental car, we heard an amplified voice shouting, "Do you want to go to a restaurant?" We turned around and saw a young girl, about ten, standing in the doorway of the house across the street and holding a megaphone. She repeated her question. She was blonde and barefoot and wore a yellow tank top and leggings.

We looked around and at each other.

"Is she talking to us?" asked my fourteen-year-old daughter, Sophia.

I shrugged my shoulders.

"A real restaurant?" my husband shouted.

"Yes!" said the girl. "A really real restaurant!" She sprinted across the street with a piece of paper in her hands and then handed it to me. I started to read and, like Proust biting into his madeleine, I was whisked back to my childhood, when my sister and I would play restaurant in our backyard and copy out elaborate menus by hand.

Here is what was on the paper:

Sómst menu

Stir egg - 550

Pasta with butter/oil - 550

Bread with butter and cheese - 300

Garlic Bread: x 1 = 100, x 5 = 500

Bread with Spam - 300

Drinks

Crystal - 200

Water - 0

Ribena - 200

Tropi - 155

Coke - 200

Children's Menu

Pasta - 250

Bread with butter - 199

Cut apple - 100

Cheerios - 55

The prices were in Icelandic króna, and so low that I immediately wished we had skipped the grocery store to eat our last supper at this restaurant instead. Iceland is expensive. The restaurant had to be taking a loss, selling everything so cheap.

Another girl—a *co-restaurateur*, apparently—appeared. She lived in the upstairs suite of the house we were staying at and had evidently alerted her friend to our presence.

I was impressed by their courage, enterprise, and near-perfect English. I was also a little jealous. My sister and I never had any customers other than our parents and the cat, and here were these girls courting strange foreigners as customers. I wondered what their parents thought of all this and noticed a dad-like figure leaving the house across the street. He looked at us and smiled before walking away down the block.

My husband, who spent his childhood weekends playing war games in the park and not putting dandelions in vases for a backyard cafe, decided not to come. He later told me that he was afraid there would be an awkward situation if we walked into the house only to find that the parents hadn't approved the plan after all.

My curiosity, not to mention good manners, made refusal impossible. Sophia agreed, but eight-year-old Sebastian said he "might come over later." I expect he was intimidated by these confident Icelandic girls.

Sophia and I followed the girls across the street and into the house, where they asked whether we wanted to sit inside or outside. The family dining room was modern Scandinavian design at its best: spacious, spare, and with beautifully finished wood everywhere, like if Ikea furniture were made with top-quality materials, and put together by a real carpenter instead of oneself. But because the weather was so good, we sat outside on the deck.

The "Bread with Spam" intrigued me. I hadn't seen Spam on a menu since 2007, when I joined the queue in front of a Spamburger stand at the Albuquerque Balloon Festival. (They ran out of Spamburgers before I got to the front of the line, which is probably for the best.)

The water, at zero króna, also looked like a good choice.

"I'll have the Bread with Spam and water, please," I said.

Our hostess paused for a moment, bit her lip, and said, "The Spam is brown. Is that okay?"

"Sure, no problem," I said.

"It's brown, but it's not old. It's new."

"Sounds good." New Spam is my favourite.

Sophia ordered a sliced apple for one hundred króna.

The two girls disappeared for a few minutes.

We waited, enjoying the warm and mellow June evening, and thought back on the year's eating. We had fallen in love with the fresh young herring in the Netherlands and the tapas lifestyle of Andalucía. In west Ireland, we discovered a passionate artisanal and locavore movement. Who knew they made an excellent chorizo in County Cork?

Iceland had also proven surprising as a culinary destination. I didn't lose my head over the "gourmet hot dogs" the online reviewers raved about, but I adored the traditional fish stew from a highway cafe and ate several helpings of the arctic char salad at a breakfast buffet, trying to figure out how to reproduce it at home.

Soon our food arrived. The apple slices were arrayed on a pretty flowered dish and the water was iced. We hadn't ordered the Cheerios, but they came as an add-on, served dry, on small square plates.

The Spam turned out to be liverwurst, which evoked pleasant memories of the previous summer in Amsterdam, where I sat on the patio of our local cafe and ate sliced liverwurst on toothpicks with mustard and drank cold wheat beer.

Sebastian turned up then, tried my Bread with Spam, and ordered some for himself.

"This is Spam?" he said. "Spam is good!"

"It's not Spam. Spam is not good. But maybe Spam is the Icelandic word for liverwurst."

I was asked to write my name down on the bill, and soon it was time to pay.

"That will be seven hundred." I handed the girls a one thousand krona note.

"Do you want change?" said the one who brought the food. Clever, she was.

"No, keep the change." The girls looked at each other with big eyes and big smiles.

"Okay, thank you for coming," said the one who had held the megaphone.

"Have a good summer!" I said, as we left.

"You're welcome. I mean… thank you!"

We walked across the street back to our house. Sophia said her apple was tart, sweet and crunchy, much better than the cheap ones we'd recently been buying. Sebastian said the restaurant was "So cute! Everyone except mass-murderers would want to go there!" This being his top rating for a dining establishment.

What do we want from our food? Beyond sustenance, I mean. For me, I think it comes down to delight and connection. Half the fun of eating stuffed mussels in Turkey was interacting with the vendors—their amusement at my pitiful Turkish and watching them feed Sebastian a few mussels by hand, *gratis*. Our favourite tapas bar in Seville was not the best one, but the one where the waiter recognized us and knew what we liked. On New Year's Eve in Paris, my already-tasty dish of ham and noodles was made exquisite by the kindness of the bistro's regulars, who generously included a tourist family in their celebration.

At Sómst, interacting with these enterprising young girls and actually being invited into their home made me feel much more connected to Icelandic people and culture than a gourmet hot dog or a trip to the Phallological Museum ever could. I briefly considered submitting a review of the restaurant to TripAdvisor, but decided against it. Sómst will remain a local secret, a great bargain, and my favourite restaurant in Europe.

RECIPE FOR A VEGETARIAN

by Jessica Kluthe

1. MEAT, GROWN ON A FARM. CUBED.

In the years before my parents knocked down some walls, our house was made of small rooms. The kitchen was a square of dark cupboards, a refinished auction-find table, and black countertops that contained jars of antique utensils, collectable tins, and small appliances. Our house—stuffed with five kids, two parents, and always open to neighbors and friends—was teeming with things and people. There was always something boiling over on the stove, being chopped, being spilled. Long after everyone would clear their plates and leave the table, I'd still be there in the kitchen: playing with my messy mousy brown hair, pressing the floral design on the end of the fork into the pad of my thumb, or using my butter knife to chop whatever it was on my plate into perfect squares.

"Just finish what's on your plate and you can go," Dad said

on Mom's instruction.

"No," I said without looking up from my burger patty food-cubes. I'd eaten the bun, the tomato, the crispy lettuce leaves. I'd had three glasses of juice. The brown cubes, now dried-out beef, would not, could not, enter my mouth.

"It's not Green Eggs and Ham, Jess," Dad said impatiently.

For most meals, I'd pull out the drawer in the table, which in another century had been used as a desk, and store the meat in there until it was safe to put it in the garbage and pile things—coffee filters, paper towel—on top. Today, they were hovering.

"Well, where did this come from?" I asked Dad as I held up a dusty brown cube to the fancy light fixture above. Earlier that week, in my grade two class we had stapled together booklets of vegetables with googley-eyed, big-toothed faces. Bright orange carrot people with mounds of curly green hair and round-bellied eggplant men with black top hats. There were fruit families: apricots holding hands with speech bubbles that said, "We're healthy," bursting out the side of their mouths and a mama banana cradling a baby banana. And as we colored, we learned that these things were grown on trees, on vines, on plants, and underground. But, nowhere in the booklet were there brown chunks, patties, or strips of meat.

"Meat is grown on farms, hun. You need it to grow strong. Puts hair on your chest," Dad said as he pulled the ice cream bowls out of the cupboard and then leaned into the open freezer.

"Grown?" I imagined a farmer, curly black hair spilling over the neckline of his coveralls, with a watering can in hand, as I lifted my fork into my mouth.

2. REMOVE THE BONES. (SAVE THEM FOR SOUP.)

Before bed, I'd walk my fingers down my ribs. I was a skinny kid—from a long line of skinny people on my dad's side of the family. My Italian grandmother, on my mom's side, would say doesn't she eat? Lit from my nightlight below, I'd stare at the framed poster of Strawberry Shortcake on my bedroom wall: "Berry Sweet" it said in red block letters. Before falling asleep, I looked at Strawberry's chubby pink body, her dimpled elbows, and sing the skipping song as I tapped against each long bone: "Strawberry shortcake, blueberry pie, who's gonna be your lucky guy?"

It happened sometime during the Strawberry years, when my bedroom walls were still bubblegum pink. That night as I felt my ribcage, pressed my fingers against the bones, I thought about my insides. The skeleton beneath my skin. The organs it caged. The tight muscles between each white bone. That day, we'd been visiting my grandparent's farm in Mearns, Alberta. We went there often; it was only twenty minutes down a bumpy country road from where we lived in town. Dad and I walked over the edge of the yard that separated where they lived—the garden, the driveway, the house—from where they worked—the barns, the wheat field, the tractor. Out back, exploring the farmyard where Dad grew up, I yanked tall quack grass from the ground and stared up at the drifting cloud shapes. We rounded a clump of thick trees, and then I saw it. A rotted-out, grey pig without a face. Its ribcage wide as one of the rusted-out cars behind the garage. We could have fit inside of it. I gasped and Dad said, "Oh. Don't look."

Later that afternoon, I gathered with my cousins in my grandparents' front room to watch TV and eat hot dogs and corn off Corelle plates. I picked at the bun, removed the kernels from the cob like a beaver, and then eyed the tube of pork.

"I'll eat that if you're not gonna," my cousin said as she reached for the boiled hot dog, thick as two fingers, pink as lips. I crossed my arms, hugged them around my ribcage, and balanced the empty plate on my knees.

3. COOK SLOW, ON LOW HEAT.

It was the kind of restaurant that felt like a basement. Even though it was a bright summer evening, the thick curtains were drawn. Dark wood paneling ran the length of the dining room and the dim lamps in the corners and the tealights on the table left everyone in shadow. A decade-old cloth napkin spread across my bare legs. We'd spent the afternoon lying out in the sun in Edmonton's Emily Murphy Park, my legs, bubbled and burnt, were peeling back like onion skin.

"Jess cooked herself today," my partner said across the table to his parents. I mumbled about sunscreen and then spread open the menu across my face. 100 per cent Alberta Beef. AAA. I skimmed for pasta. Nope. Chicken? Nope.

I squinted across the table at my partner's parents who recited the appetizers and asked if anyone wanted to share. The waiter came by with a cart and a big silver bowl between his arm and hip.

"Our famous Caesar salad?"

He balanced a bright white egg in this palm and then cracked it on the edge of the bowl. The thick yolk slid down the side, plunked down onto the lettuce and wiggled. I reread the menu.

My 8 oz. sirloin was cooked at the table along with everyone else's chunks, patties, and strips of meat. The waiter explained the process, the low heat, just when each piece should be turned. Talked about why the beef in Alberta is best, what the animals eat. Once plated, my cooked carrots and fried mushrooms soaked in the deep red juices. I seesawed my knife through it, pressed my fork down to squeeze out the liquids, and I chewed. I talked about the weather with the bite of steak in my cheek. I chewed some more, thick strings in my teeth—and when something squirted out, I leaned down and spit it out into my napkin. I folded the cloth around it, and tucked the warm package under my thigh.

"Yes, please box it up."

He balanced my plate on top of his flat palm and turned toward the kitchen. When he returned, he smiled and placed the Styrofoam box in front of me. There, on the lid, in blue ink, was a cartoon cow. Big googley-eyes. A row of spiky hair. Out of the side of the cow's mouth, in block letters, it said, "MOO!"

4. LABEL LEFTOVERS.

"It's natural to eat meat. Part of the life cycle," Dad recited as he carved through the stretchy skin of the chicken breast on his plate. "Those plants chopped up on your plate were living too. Same difference."

I nodded, eyebrows up, lips tight. My family, crammed around the table, smirked, and passed a bowl of oddly shaped garden strawberries around the table.

I turned the white-splotched berry over in my fingers before dropping it to my plate. "Plants grow, then you yank them out of the ground and their life is over, too," Dad continued.

I imagined placing the strawberry on the BBQ grill just out the patio doors behind my parents. I imagined Strawberry Shortcake leg kick open the heavy lid, jam her elbow out the side and jump down.

My younger brother stopped texting, placed his cellphone next to his fork and spoon, and entered the conversation.

"Yeah, plant killer. You're just a vag-a-tar-ian now."

The table erupted first with gasps then with head-back, eyes-up, laughter.

I imagined Strawberry Shortcake bursting through the doors and biting into my brother's skinny chicken legs.

THE DEVOLUTION
OF CAKE

by Angela Palm

EXPLODING space matter birthed galaxies. Mud-dwelling amoebae evolved into flagellated organisms. Amniotic-drenched kittens tumbled from the flexed hind legs of cats. Duly, life slogs from life. The word *placenta* recoiled, too, from an omphalos. Its etymological birth is rooted in Latin, meaning flat cake, and in the Greek word *plakoenta*, referring to a flat surface. At altar, the ancient Romans offered *placenta*, a thin, sweet cake having nothing to do with bloody afterbirth, as a sacrifice to their pantheon of gods. Among the beseeched was Ceres, a goddess whose lordly realms included motherly love and agriculture, fertility and rites for the dead. Made of layered honey, cheeses, bay leaves, and pastry, *placenta* preceded the modern conception of cake. More like a cross between pizza and baklava, placenta was fashioned with intent, offered in earnest, and consumed consciously and rarely.

• • •

I was nearly eight months pregnant. A humid one hundred degrees marked the typical start to another Indiana summer. Numbly, I arranged plastic utensils on the table where the catered food would soon go, manipulated the dyed carnations in their foam-filled containers. They would not stop looking fake and pitiful despite my efforts. Everything and everyone was sweating: the gallon of Countrytime lemonade on the table, my father's round stomach as he aligned rows of folding chairs, my own stretched abdomen. *Lucky*, I thought to my unborn boy, as I jabbed another stem into green foam, *at least you get a continuous bath*. I never spoke to my future son directly, out loud, like the mothers to-be did in movies. I tried once and felt foolish. *Maybe it's a sign that I'm not cut out for this*, I wondered to myself. I had been wondering that for a while. When I asked my mother about her experiences as a new mom to my infant self, she only vaguely remembered it. So as with everything else I had learned, I read books and academic papers on pregnancy, childbirth, and childcare to educate myself. I would do everything right with this baby, even though I had no track record to support that as a probably outcome. A selfish part of me wished I would go into labor right there, ending every insufferable part of that day. But, no. Sacrifice: that was the order of motherhood.

My mother and her three sisters, who were at once the creators and the coordinators of chaos, had tasked me with picking up the cake for the memorial service scheduled for later that day in my parents' pole barn. I did what they expected of me as quietly as possible, which wasn't even necessary because they only heard themselves speak. For years, my cousin Mandi and I had watched them like this. We would sit back and wonder who the adults really were—them or us? We'll be different, we would always say. We'll be the kinds of mothers we always wanted, we said, as I think most people approaching parenting do. We would correct the things that had gone wrong for us. We would never scream, never spank. Never bring too many step-fathers into the picture. We would never stifle our children's natural selves, never mold them into our own likeness as if parenting were a godlike position.

"Make sure you get a receipt," my mom said, "so you can submit it to the estate for reimbursement."

"To the *estate*? For cake?" I asked. The woman *in memoriam* was my grandmother and she had died three months earlier, so the immediacy of her death had waned. The plucking of Gram's existence from ours had dulled. Somehow, it had taken that long for her five children to pull together a formal memorial.

"What? People do it all the time," my mom replied. As a probate paralegal, she would have known. But with respect to my Gram's estate, which as far as I could tell extended to the contents of seven bins and boxes, it seemed absurd. Plus, I could afford it. My mom could afford. Did she really need to borrow the minor expense against the estate, which would only cut into her siblings' shares? It was just another of the many bricks that built the wall between us.

• • •

In Medieval Europe, desserts were a novelty largely limited to the upper class and royalty. Honey commonly provided sweetness, and nuts were added for texture and flavor in several European regions. Knowledge about this time period's cakes comes from surviving recipe books and instruction manuals. Measurements of ingredients were precise. Cooking was a long and delicate process; stone fires required stoking and achieving consistent heating throughout a single dish was difficult.

. . .

Before Gram went into the ICU, before hospice, before her faded eyes looked past the nurses and died, my mother was barely speaking to her. Before that, she had been tersely calling Gram "Mother." But she had had a change of heart and began referring to her lovingly as "Mama" when Gram entered hospice care. Before her death became inevitable, she rolled her eyes while on the phone, barely listening to Gram's catalogue of ailments. My grandmother had been through many fatal false alarms—childhood through adulthood, beginning with contracting polio at age eight and spending a year in an iron lung. Later it was heart problems, resulting in several surgeries. Round after round of pneumonia that would kill her, but never did. Though there were many things my mother had helped Gram with over the years as her health wavered and restored, toward the end she seemed often to ignore her requests for help around her tiny, subsidized apartment. Ignored her imploring for company once she was in the nursing home. Not every time, of course, but enough to make it seem like a weight she'd rather throw to the ground. But my mother was always tallying things up. She said to me, "I've put in more than my fair share. I bought her new furniture when she had that apartment. She ruined it with her chain smoking. I bring her that special yogurt she likes. Do my sisters do that? Does Pat do that?" At that point, I was to say, "No, you do it all. They ought to take on more of your great burden." My Gram had always said, "Those who can do help those who can't do," and I considered reminding my mother of that, but I said nothing because the cost of a few yogurts and a loveseat didn't seem an unreasonable currency for the result: continued dignity, small comfort. *Let her complain*, I told myself. *No judgement. Not your problem.* I had stopped trying to change my parents. Instead of fighting them, I had simply stopped engaging in the conflict and reserved my thoughts for people to whom they mattered.

I don't blame my mom entirely for her lack of sympathy. I understood the frustration. My grandmother, though I loved her dearly, was a difficult, secretive, and deceitful person. Gram had tried to have my mother arrested a few months back. My mother had stored Gram's purse at her house rather than risk leaving it in a hospital cubby for what ended up being a two-week hospital stay. Gram called the police from her hospital bed to report that my mother had stolen it, despite the fact that she was her power of attorney and paid Gram's bills while she was hospitalized. Case workers and police officers scrutinized and questioned her. But in the purse, she found that Gram had stashed the rubber tourniquet tubing that she'd stolen from the hospital when the nurses weren't looking. This confirmed what she already knew was true—what nobody would discuss out loud or tell Gram's healthcare providers: my grandmother had been shooting up her pain meds. Even when they learned that Gram's current health complication was a blood infection, no one offered this information to the doctors. It was a symptom of this family's disease: masking undesirable truths to save face and a preoccupation with appearing happy rather than experiencing what was actually happening.

Before I left to get the cake, I saw my mother write on Facebook, "Here's a picture of my dear Mama." Then, she said to someone on the phone, "Are you coming to Mama's memorial?" At fifty years old, she was a small child again, grasping for the safety of her mother's thighs. I wanted to hug her, but the wall had grown too high for that. As I watched her across the kitchen, I wondered who my mother was before she had children, before she was dealing with the care of her own mother on a day to day basis. The Internet, and Facebook in particular, was an extension of place. It gathered people together from the past, many faces from many different places. It opened another realm of existence, where one could be a slightly better, slightly more presentable version of one's messy self. It gave us a place to love our mothers the way we wished to love them, to forget, at least within the space of the Internet filament, that they were flawed; to forget that we ourselves were flawed. The Internet, in many ways, was a happy, pretend place. Or some version of the truth. Just another real-life story that was rivered by the banks of our choosing.

• • •

In the 1700s, bakers began omitting yeast from their cake recipes. They gathered eggs in the early daylight hours, and later beat them into the batter with their well-trained hands. Conical corsets mirrored conical-shaped cake towers, or perhaps the other way around. Liqueurs were baked into hoop-bound cake forms by women sporting panniers beneath their frocks. There was the sense that the layering of both cakes and women's clothing went on forever, compressing their innards into a tiny infinity.

While leavening agents and the shape of cakes were changing in the eighteenth century, the social circumstances of eating them were not. Trade vessels bearing spices offered a complexity of flavor for those who could afford to buy them. Lard and sweetmeats added savory notes to cakes served at ceremonies, weddings, and religious holiday celebrations.

• • •

Before Gram went loopy in conversations and began dozing off mid-bite at lunch, in retrospect the side effects of the medication misuse, we did regular things. We splashed poolside and shared the joy of watching Patrick Swayze dance on TV. There was the pleasant routine of feeding chickens and gathering eggs. We spent time assessing their different textures and colors and weights. Flecked brown, smooth white, a touch of green—all of them splendid little miracles. We made cherry cheesecake from scratch with my mother watching us from the doorway, smiling a little, pretending she wasn't trying to watch the *how* of it, though I saw her recording the steps in her mind: *flour, butter, forks, fingers.* But she must have forgotten, because she never did show me how to make a crust, let alone a whole cheesecake. Birthday cakes came from a box at our house; there was no ritual. Each year I asked for rainbow chip frosting and my mother forgot and added rainbow sprinkles. *The chips*, I'd say. *I wanted chips*. Eventually, I gave up the expectation altogether and smiled at whatever cake was presented. But inside I felt myself getting further from them. My parents did not want to know me. Not really.

I had to figure out baking on my own, later, when I had my own kitchen. Like a sorcerer, I'd closed my eyes and envisioned Gram's process, laid my hands across a carton of eggs waiting for them to speak to me, then turned to the Internet to fill the gaps in my memory.

By my best accounting, my grandmother was overwhelmed as a mostly single mother of five, and she was busy drifting into and out of a slew of marriages that didn't last. A certain detachment from her primary role as a parent seemed a mechanism for survival, perhaps her only one. In many ways, she did a remarkable job with her children, but they each have their irreparable marks. From the perspective of a generation removed, a generation resulting of aunts who had also set out to "make things better" for their own children, I can see how it happened: in moments. In the moment, for example, that you choose not to teach your daughter to make a crust from scratch because there's too much to do already, too many mouths to feed in quick succession, and not enough time to teach any of them how they will later feed their own children—let alone themselves. (When that time does come, they'll do the best they can with canned potatoes and precooked meats, fast food, and Chef Boyardee.) It happens in the moment you realize that, instead of proper food, your eight-year-old daughter only knows how to make a good highball. (Go easy on the ginger ale, extra ice.) In another moment, you discover that your adult daughter cannot bake a cake and must, instead, dump boxed powders into a bowl for her own daughter's birthday, which stings a little. Your granddaughter learns to crack the egg, lick the bowl, and nothing more. My relationship with my own mother would develop similarly—the breakdown between mothers and daughters on her side of the family like an inheritable disease. It began with mistaking sprinkles for chips.

The aged reliably refocus their energy and intentions near the end of life, quietly wishing they had realized sooner that all the previous moments had been important. That the weight of the sum of those moments had always been moving at a slow velocity toward a singular reckoning, like a star burned out years earlier, its light still visible in the present. The illusion almost cruel. The heavy moments, noticed too late, anchored you too soon in a chair from which a certified nursing assistant spoon-feeds you; the lighter ones kept you afloat for another season of watching pussy willows bud.

The sum of my mother's moments had yet to be reconciled; the weight of my own were even further away. The weight of dumping boxed powder versus the value of personal instruction remained unmeasured, as did the weight of self versus other and of too much versus not enough. But the stars had already begun their burnout.

• • •

Baking soda, made of the chemical compound sodium bicarbonate, was first used by the ancient Egyptians in preserving their dead for the journey to the afterlife. Fast forward several thousand years to the Industrial Revolution, where together baking soda and baking powder simplified cake baking, forever changing baking and the culture of baked-good consumption. Flour was bleached, refined. Thinned. These innovations resulted in cakes that were accessible to the everyman in his everyday life, made by his everyday wife. Thus, competition in the boxed-cake market began and any given day could become an occasion for cake. Perhaps this is where the burnout began, when mothers and daughters who had once relied upon one another's assistance from kitchen to table, creating a legacy of knowledge around sacred celebrations, could now pursue other paths. They could be other things, to themselves and to one another.

• • •

Many meetings happened with respect to Gram, the aging process in 2010 navigated by committee. When she was alive and careening toward death, the five of them met with doctors and psychiatrists and caseworkers about her care at the nursing home, about what it would take to commit her, about which of them she could live with. (None, as it turned out.) I imagined massive conference tables, doors closing for privacy. Pens poised over notebooks, all as Gram lay dying. The private meetings, ones without doctors, were about the morphine addiction she'd developed in response to her post-polio pain. About the horror of finding used needles and burned-up spoons hidden in the plastic cubbies that rolled around Gram's bathroom floor to make room for her walker. About the doped-up twenty-two-year-old she met outside of a grocery store who started sleeping on her couch and stealing her social security and eating her key lime yogurts—a meeting whose details I can't help but try to conjure in my mind. Did Gram approached him or he her? Did she use slang in her corralling of the disaffected? How had she acquired this particular vernacular? What did the words *shoot up* sound like in my grandmother's dentured mouth? Like marbles? Silk? Putty? How did they stick against her teeth, and did she redden with shame or was she brazen and unafraid when she spoke them? How, exactly, did a nearly eighty-year-old woman entangle herself in such a situation? What were the logistics of it?

Now the meetings were about planning Gram's memorial, about catering, about the division of her seven bins and boxes, about who would speak first. About cake.

In the grocery store parking lot, I sat in the air conditioning of my car for longer than was environmentally responsible. I looked at my face in the mirror and dabbed my swollen cheeks with powder. I applied lip gloss that was too pink for my skin tone. I was a terrible pregnant woman. From the beginning it had been clear I was not made for it. I'd had hyperemesis gravidarum, that constant illness in early pregnancy which Princess Kate Middleton's pregnancy had shed light on, legitimizing for the public what sufferers of the condition had known all along: *no, really, my morning sickness is much worse than yours.* After that passed, finally, I was irritable and uncomfortable as my hips had shifted and tilted, making exercise almost impossible, let alone standing or sitting comfortably. I emerged from the car and plunge into the heat, feeling huge and unwieldy in my pregnant body. I looked left and right, not for cars, but for familiar faces. I'd be mortified if I saw anyone I had gone to high school with, mainly because I was popping into the grocery store on a Friday, eight months pregnant, as if I was just running an errand in the middle of an aimless day and didn't have a job, which was not the case. As if I did this all the time. As if it were *my* grocery store, pregnancy my only accomplishment.

I wove my way through shelved loaves of bread and rows of green, red, and yellow condiments, careful not to look up at anyone, and arrived breathlessly at the bakery department.

"I'm picking up a cake for McCann," I said to the bakery attendant, who looked a little too young to know me. I leaned on the glass countertop, a small measure of relief. "Or Dye. Actually, it might be under Williams."

I hadn't asked what name the cake would be listed under. I could not recall which last name my grandmother had died with—she had had so many. All the women in our family had married multiple times, except for my own mother, who had been married just once—to my father. Between my grandmother and her four daughters, they had been married fourteen times, collectively. That I knew of. There had been uncles whose names I had already forgotten.

"All right. There are two, actually." He retrieved them from a rolling cart and presented them to me. "Just take these up to the register when you're ready to pay," he said, sliding a hand-written receipt across the counter to me.

"Thanks," I said. There was an assortment of remainder donuts in the glass case below my forearms. "Can I have a cream puff, too? Or whatever those are called," I said, pointing down at the mounds of curlicue pastry and white fluff.

He smiled at me with mild affection and reddened,

assumingly because I was enormously pregnant and adding donuts to my cake order. But that was not why I was buying it. Gram had always kept fresh cream puffs at her house when I visited as a kid. They weren't my favorite, but they had been hers, and right then that was good enough for me.

"Sure," he said, stifling a laugh.

"You know what they say about a pregnant woman's appetite." I winked at him, which was not something I would normally do. I feared it might constitute harassment—was this kid even eighteen? I wanted to stop talking and sit down as soon as possible.

"Um," he said. "Yeah. Oh, I need you to check the cakes to make sure everything's the way you ordered it."

I popped open the box of the first cake. The frosting was white with accents in Gram's favorite color, orange. The words HONORED and LOVED were scrawled above and below the frosting screen print of a young Donna, as if the all-caps somehow made the words truer, an embodiment of redemption. They reminded me of one of the last things she had told me. "There's a lot they don't tell you about getting old. Your own children won't take you in after everything you've done for them. In the end, you'll be alone." In reality, she had lived with nearly every one of her children for a short time—quickly exasperating their emotional resources. At one point, I told her she could live with me, but she had declined. "Just knowing you mean it is enough," she'd said. Later, my mother got calls from the nursing home that she had escaped. Once, twice, three times. The police would find her a mile away trudging through traffic, the tennis balls of her walker worn and molested by the pavement. I thought for a minute about licking off the HONORED and the D in LOVED, and then asking the bakery boy to write TOUGH instead. That would have been more accurate. But tough love was more complex when the subject was your elderly mother, or grandmother. And nobody wrote books or offered weekly support groups on how to manage that. It was one more slanted truth, one more reality buried, one more place where we could mitigate the circumstances of our real lives.

In the second box was another cake with another frosting-printed picture and another all-caps message that read DONNA-MITE. I sighed. It was absurd. "Yeah, this looks about right."

"Great. Enjoy your cream puff," he said with a laugh.

"You have to Get Smart," Gram would say, tapping her temple. "That's how to win at life." She wasn't wrong. But she was silly, taking her made-up axioms to unexpected degrees of seriousness. She had always said she wanted it written on her headstone when she died: Get Smart Lives Here. Would they do it? I wondered as I approached the check-out area. Would her kids actually do that? I carefully selected a line whose cashier I was certain would not know me—my disdain for this town almost crippling. Lately, when I approached the exit from the highway on a visit home, anxiety would kick in, a physical reaction to the mere act of returning for even a short visit. I paid and waddled out to my car to sit in the air conditioning again.

"Fuck this cake," I said, looking right at it as if it could hear me. Seeing her face in edible sugar didn't sit right with me. It was not the face I knew. The face I knew was aged and lovely, framed in fake, bleach-blonde hair. I did not know this smooth-smiling woman with dark hair. I'd heard only rumors about the secrets it held—was it true that she had fed my mother's father rat poison? If, when refreshments were served, I was offered my Gram's young-self face, I might throw up. How could I possibly eat a dead woman's cake face?

I took the cream puff out of its bag and ate the whole thing. With my mouth full of homage, I said again with gusto, "Fuck. This. Cake."

• • •

As unionization swept the North American business landscape, women entered the workforce and dual income became a necessity for many families rather than a rarity. Disposable income and block chunks of weekend leisure time redefined western culture. Families began going out for meals more frequently and the restaurant industry boomed. Cakes and other baked sweets were commoditized twofold: A diverse range of desserts created with both creative and commercial intention offered restaurant-goers many après-meal selections; cake tradeshows held in city conference centers further commercialized the cake industry, inviting private shop owners and chain restaurant marketers alike to invest in the offerings. The culture of sweets was alive and well, but it looked nothing like its history. The commonness of baking institutional knowledge that had been passed down from one generation to the next was now scarce.

• • •

Four sisters gathered around a nondescript kitchen table to discuss their mother's memorial proceedings, which would commence in a few hours. Where at one time the sisters might have engaged in a silent, physical mourning as they dusted pans and folded eggs into the batter that would rise into cake, now they only waited and pecked at one another's opinions.

Maureen: Cathleen will speak first. She's good at that kind of thing.

Cathleen: D'you guys want me to?

Maureen: Well, do you want to?

Cathleen: I don't mind, if that's what you're asking.

Colleen: Do you or don't you?

Cathleen: Yes.

Colleen: Yes you mind? Or yes you'll do it?

Cathleen: I'll do it. I want to do it.

Colleen: After you, it'll be Maury.

Cathleen: But what about Colleen? Shouldn't she go next? She's the oldest.

Carleen: Then I'll be last. I'm always last. How about *I* go first—

Colleen: No, Car. Kathy goes first, then oldest to youngest.

Carleen: Youngest to oldest. I'm tired of being left out of everything. There'll be nothing left to say by the time it's my turn.

Maureen: What about Patrick?

Cathleen: What about him? He's not here.

Maureen: Well, should we get him on speaker or something?

Colleen: No, not for a memorial. You don't do that. Jesus, Maury.

Maureen: Well, excuse me for wanting to include our only brother.

Cathleen: I don't appreciate you taking the Lord's name in vain, Colleen.

Colleen: I'm fucking Buddhist, Cathleen.

Watching this group of women trying to organize themselves to perform one of the most ancient human rituals frightened me. Somewhere along the line, our branch of the family tree must have been severed from the source trunk that held all the basics of lineage: rites of passage, burial rituals, birth ceremonies.

"Here's the cake," I said once they quieted down. I set the boxes in front of them on the table.

My mother popped open their tops, and she and her sisters peered into my grandmother's frosting face like it was a wishing well. When they weren't talking, their faces were mostly the same: all lips and eyes with just a suggestion in the brow of being maybe-or-maybe-not-of-the-same-paternity. After they stopped crying, my mom held out her hand. "Did you get the receipt?"

I took it out of my pocket and handed it to her, my breath catching with the strain of a false contraction.

• • •

In 2009, a reality TV show called *Cake Boss* premiered on cable. Its documentary approach zoomed in on the day-to-day business of running a family-owned cake bakery. Based in Hoboken, New Jersey, the show stars Italian-American Buddy Valastro. His team of bakers and staff, most of whom are related to Valastro by blood or marriage, creates monstrous cakes in the shape of craps tables, football fields, New York City, animals, cars—you name it—that often stretch the length of a kitchen table or more. In his kitchen, Valastro's big personality and a string of catastrophes among the staff keep viewers engaged.

• • •

The whole time the speeches were going, four given live and one speaker-phoned in (after all, my mother would have her way), I thought about the boy from the grocery store who laughed about the cream puff. After an hour, I felt like I was going to faint and they were still talking, so I stood in the yard and watched the scene from there. I sat in the grass, took my shoes off, and turned the hose on to a slow flow to cool my legs.

They had everyone who knew Gram that was still alive seated in rows of folding chairs in the barn. I watched sweat rings form on their backs. Drops of it rolled down the red slopes of bald, speckled heads. Ladies fanned themselves and wiped sweat from their brows. My dad's drop-down golf net was pinned up and secured above them, hanging over their heads like a trapeze act's safety net. A slideshow happened, then music. People grew restless, and none of the sisters seemed to notice or care. Eulogies were not for the dead, after all. They were for the living. With the hose still going and my feet almost numb from the cold, I stared into the cornfield that surrounded my parents' property until I could hear it—the far off rustling of barely-moving leaves and tassels that make a wet *sh-sh* sound. For a moment, it was the loveliest sound I had ever heard. It was a brief, bright connection to some bit of former life I'd lived. For a few seconds, I remembered Corey. Marcus, Mandi. All of us together and laughing like crazy without a thought as to what our futures might hold. Our surroundings—the river, the fields—just scenery instead of associative icons of the things that happened to us later. Like a sea-weary sailor to a siren, I was ready to drown myself in that one sweet memory. We were dispersed all over the country now. Dispelled. The corn stopped making noise as the second hour of speech-giving passed, and I shifted my attention to my cell phone. I looked up *cream puff* in the Urban Dictionary. There were a couple of possible uses, both involving the precise deposit of male gametes onto the female body. *That little bastard,* I thought, *no wonder he was laughing.*

I felt terrible about the people sitting in their drenched clothes in the barn. I was half-expecting someone to pass out, when they were finally released from the speeches and welcomed to start eating face-cake. I went into the house to lie down in the air conditioning, put a pillow over my face, and screamed. I forgot that the baby could hear me.

· · ·

Cake pops, which were gaining popularity as a wedding cake alternative and birthday party fare in the early twenty-first century, are made by scooping dollops of batter into form pans, inserting cardboard lollipop-style sticks into each pop before baking, and then coating the cooled "cakes" in candy frosting.

The finished product could be eaten in a single bite—by literally popping them into one's mouth. With over 107 million search results for recipes on Google, the trendy desserts promised to stick around for a while.

• • •

A few weeks after the memorial, my son was born via emergency C-section—more proof that my body could not hack motherhood. The first thought I had was *we should be dead. Two hundred years ago, we would have been dead. A hundred years ago, dead.* I wanted to live. I wanted me and my baby to live. Don't get me wrong. But I questioned the privilege of life at all costs, both on the birthing and on the dying ends of the spectrum. What right did I have? What were the costs? Was I really meant to live? Or had medical advancements circumvented fate? Later, I would discover that the monetary costs were in the neighborhood of thirty thousand dollars for a ten-minute C-section and aftercare. The number of times my grandmother's life was saved before it finally expired flashed in my mind. How much had been spent to keep her alive that long, after polio had spit her back out? And what were the other costs?

Deep in my lungs, as they stuffed my organs back into my abdomen while my husband watched, I felt a connection to the women who had labored generations before me and not made it through. Certain they had gathered around my bedside for the event, I shared a ghostly moment with their blank faces as oxygen was drawn into my blood and filtered out through my body. I'd been spared.

Then, instead of giving the boy they'd sprung from my womb with a knife to me, a pair of gloved hands held him up to my face like a caught fish and then swept him away in blur of motion.

Hours later, I woke up in a room, without a baby, trying and failing to remember his tiny face. With my eyes out of focus, I registered my husband, who was asleep somewhere near me. The smell of blood, singed skin, sweat, and must filled my nose, which was all wrong because I should have been smelling my son's head. I had read that the top of a baby's head gives off pheromones that drive the instincts for motherly love. But no one was smelling my baby's head—its scent was evaporating into nothing, and my maternal instinct was quickly going with it. Alarms sounded throughout my body, warning me that his entire future might crumble if I didn't smell his head immediately. Unable to move my lower half, I leaned over to hit the nurse button, one, twice, three times, until a woman appeared in the doorway. Before it was explained to me why on earth I had not yet seen the child that was cut out of my stomach, a hospital representative stood in front of me with a clipboard. The nurse had not responded.

"And would you like the hospital photographer to take pictures of the baby?" she asked.

"What? No."

She marked something down on her clipboard. "And would you like a birthday cake delivered to your room? We have chocolate or vanilla. No, out of vanilla today. Just chocolate." She yawned and poised her pen over the clipboard again.

"A birthday cake? No, it's five in the morning. I want to see my baby." I tried not to curse at her because she was just doing her job.

When they finally rolled him in, I tried to nurse him, but his mouth was lazy. Already, his innate sense to search blindly for his mother with his mouth had waned, nature's reflexes having been disrupted by the surgery and the hospital staff. Already, I failed him. What he managed to eat, he threw up. Again and again. I was assured by two doctors that this was normal, but I knew it was not and asked for a third. I could tell by their eyes that I was a nuisance, that they'd rather be sleeping, but what else could I do? There was nothing to pray to; there was no matriarch to whom I could defer; there were no ceremonies to perform. My grandmother was gone. My mother did not even remember this part. The nurses were already busy with the next mother and child down the hall. My body had made it clear it would not accept motherhood without a fight. There was only me and him, the whisper of instinct, and a stack of books that would guide me.

THE CHEFS

DEB FLEISCHMAN'S recent work appears in *Neutrons/Protons*, *Vermoxie*, and *1966*. Deb co-founded Write Mondays, a writing workshop for high school students in Vermont. She holds a B.S. in Political Science from M.I.T. and an MFA from Vermont College of Fine Arts. @debfleischman

BRIANNA GOLDBERG is a writer and radio producer from Toronto with credits in *The Walrus*, *Jezebel*, CBC and beyond. Brianna spent a few years living in the Caribbean and West Africa, where she freelanced on topics ranging from lingerie trends to domestic terrorism. @b_goldberg

MAGGIE DOWNS is a writer based in Palm Springs, California. Her work has appeared in the *Washington Post*, *Los Angeles Times*, the BBC, and *Paste*, among others. You can follow her on Twitter or visit her often-neglected website. @downsanddirty

TERI VLASSOPOULOS is the Cookbookslut columnist for Bookslut. Her novel, *Escape Plans* (Invisible Publishing) is forthcoming in October 2015. She lives and writes in Toronto, and her favourite meal is breakfast. @terki

VIVEK SHRAYA is a Toronto-based artist. Vivek's body of work includes ten albums, four short films and three books. A three-time Lambda Literary Award finalist, Vivek's books have been used as textbooks at several post-secondary institutions, and his debut novel, *She of the Mountains*, was named one of The Globe and Mail's Best Books of 2014. @vivekshraya

JANE CAMPBELL'S work has appeared in *Grain*, *Revolver* and *The Impressment Gang*. She recently finished a non-fiction book about her experiences growing up fat and losing weight as an adult. She lives in Vancouver, BC with her husband and cat. @janelindsaycamp

LAUREN RAZAVI is a British-Iranian feature writer and foreign reporter for publications such as *The Guardian*, *New Statesman* and *VICE*. She studied the MA in creative writing (non-fiction) at the University of East Anglia, graduating with merit in 2014. For more, visit Lauren's website and blog. @LaurenRazavi

Originally from Sydney, ROSA VALERIE CAMPBELL now lives in London. This year her work has featured in *The Letters Page*, *Litro*, *Noted Festival*, *East End Literary Salon*, *Hoot Review*, *Freight Books* anthology and others. She loves hot coffee and has just finished her first novel. @rrrosavalerie

CINDY MATTHEWS lives in Bruce County, Canada. Her fiction has appeared in Canada, US, UK, and Australia. Her essays have been shortlisted in the 2014 *Event Creative Non-Fiction Contest* and in the 2015 *NOWW Creative Non-Fiction Contest*. For more, visit her website. @Matthec1957

DAVID BURGA is a Peruvian born Canadian geologist and writer. He lives in Mississauga with his family and is currently finishing his first novel. @davideburga

MADELEINE LEZNOFF graduated from The University of Western Ontario with a degree in media studies and writing. She currently lives in Toronto where she's a social media manager and copywriter by day. She spends her nights perfecting the blintz and is happy her writing debut involves food.

DEE HOBSBAWN-SMITH earned her MFA in Writing at the University of Saskatchewan. Her debut poetry collection, *Wildness Rushing In*, (Hagios Press, 2014) was a finalist for two SK Book Awards. *What Can't Be Undone* (Thistledown Press, 2015) is her first short fiction collection. dee also writes at The Curious Cook.

ALISA GORDANEER writes poetry and creative nonfiction, and serves as president of the Creative Nonfiction Collective Society. Her newest book, *Still Hungry* (Signature Editions), explores our complicated relationships with food. She lives in Victoria, BC. @gordaneer

TANYA R. WARD is a Toronto-based writer and teacher. She is a graduate of the University of Toronto and York University with an M.A. in philosophy. She is currently working on a collection of short fiction. @jack_and_i

ROBYN RYLE has to call her mother every time she cans tomatoes to ask how long to let them boil. She has essays and stories at *CALYX Journal*, *Gawker*, and *Midwestern Gothic* among others. @RobynRyle

REBECA DUNN-KRAHN is an eater, traveler and mom. Her story "The Third Lesson We Learned In Turkey" appeared in *Chance Encounters: Travel Tales from Around the World* published by World Traveler Press. She lives in Victoria, BC. @rebecadk

JESSICA KLUTHE (full-time vegetarian and part-time vegan) teaches creative writing at MacEwan University. She holds an MFA in Writing from the University of Victoria and is the author of the book Rosina, The Midwife. In her spare time, she volunteers for a local animal rescue. @jessicakluthe

ANGELA PALM is the author of *Riverine: A Memoir from Anywhere but Here*, recipient of the 2014 Graywolf Press Nonfiction Prize. Palm owns Ink + Lead Literary Services and is the editor of the anthology *Please Do Not Remove*. @angpalm

AMANDA LEDUC is the nonfiction editor for Little Fiction | Big Truths. Her stories and essays can be found in The Rumpus, The Toast, ELLE Canada, and StoryQuarterly, among others. Her debut novel is *The Miracles of Ordinary Men* (ECW Press). @amandaleduc

TROY PALMER is the creative direction and managing editor at Little Fiction | Big Truths. He is also a writer, music snob and fan of frequently losing sports teams. He currently lives and rarely sleeps in Toronto. @troy_palmer

ACKNOWLEDGEMENTS

Thank you Matt, Jeremy, Adam and everyone at Inkshares, and thank you to all who helped get this book funded. Your generous support made these pages happen.

Special thanks to all of the writers for trusting us with their work for sharing their deeply personal, and at times mouth-watering, stories with us.

Shout out to Vanessa Christensen for the much-needed editing and proofreading help and to Brianna Goldberg and Tanya Ward, aka The Unofficial Nomfiction Street Team, for their support on the ground.

Nomfiction would not exist if not for the ever-scheming and food-loving Amanda Leduc. Merci.

Thank YOU for reading.
—Troy Palmer, Managing Editor, Little Fiction | Big Truths

littlefiction.com
@Little_Fiction

A donation was made to the Daily Bread Food Bank in Toronto on behalf of every submission we received. Please support your local food banks if you can.

Image and Icon credits

All title icons from The Noun Project (thenounproject.com), used under Creative Commons Attribution 3.0

Images created by:

Claire Jones ("Arancini" and "How To Preserve Food For The Winter"), Gilad Fried ("Catfish"), Creative Stall ("Discomfort Food" and "Pomegranates"), Pham Thi Dieu Linh ("Messy" and "Feed The Birds"), Marco Olgio ("Fat Free" and "Bird in the Hand"), Catherine Please ("Red Beets Mingle With Potato Skins" and "The Devolution Of Cake"), Maya Irvine ("The Dinner Party"), Dmitry Baranovksiy ("Two Tables"), Alfonso Melolonta Urbán ("Handmade"), Matt Brooks ("Nil By Mouth"), chiccabubble ("And The Spoon Ran Away With The Trash"), Blake Thompson ("The Last Supper"), Aha-Soft ("Recipe For A Vegetarian"), Sylvain Amatoury (cover fork).

LIST OF PATRONS

This book was made possible in part by the following grand patrons, or "Prix Fixe" supporters, who preordered the book on Inkshares.com. Thank you.

Adam Gomolin

Alisa Gordaneer

Amanda Leduc

Angela Palm

Avalon Marissa Radys

Beth Gilstrap

Cynthia Matthews

David Burga

Jane Boyle

Kelvin Kong

Margherita Sanita

Maureen G. Henderson

Michelle Gillis

Michelle Palmer

Rebeca Dunn-Krahn

Ria Voros

Robyn Ryle

Tanya Ward

Troy Palmer

INKSHARES

Inkshares is a crowdfunded book publisher. We democratize publishing by having readers select the books we publish—we edit, design, print, distribute, and market any book that meets a preorder threshold.

Interested in making a book idea come to life? Visit inkshares.com to find new book projects or to start your own.

Printed in the USA
CPSIA information can be obtained
at www.ICGtesting.com
JSHW022337140824
68134JS00019B/1538